EXPLORING SCIENCE
WITH YOUNG CHILDREN

SAGE was founded in 1965 by Sara Miller McCune to support the dissemination of usable knowledge by publishing innovative and high-quality research and teaching content. Today, we publish over 900 journals, including those of more than 400 learned societies, more than 800 new books per year, and a growing range of library products including archives, data, case studies, reports, and video. SAGE remains majority-owned by our founder, and after Sara's lifetime will become owned by a charitable trust that secures our continued independence.

Los Angeles | London | New Delhi | Singapore | Washington DC

EXPLORING SCIENCE
WITH YOUNG CHILDREN
A DEVELOPMENTAL PERSPECTIVE

TERRY RUSSELL & LINDA MCGUIGAN

Los Angeles | London | New Delhi
Singapore | Washington DC

Los Angeles | London | New Delhi
Singapore | Washington DC

SAGE Publications Ltd
1 Oliver's Yard
55 City Road
London EC1Y 1SP

SAGE Publications Inc.
2455 Teller Road
Thousand Oaks, California 91320

SAGE Publications India Pvt Ltd
B 1/I 1 Mohan Cooperative Industrial Area
Mathura Road
New Delhi 110 044

SAGE Publications Asia-Pacific Pte Ltd
3 Church Street
#10-04 Samsung Hub
Singapore 049483

Editor: Amy Jarrold
Assistant editor: George Knowles
Production editor: Tom Bedford
Copyeditor: Salia Nessa
Proofreader: Katie Forsythe
Indexer: Charmian Parkin
Marketing manager: Dilhara Attygalle
Cover design: Wendy Scott
Typeset by: C&M Digitals (P) Ltd, Chennai, India
Printed in India at Replika Press Pvt Ltd

Library of Congress Control Number: 2015946030

British Library Cataloguing in Publication data

A catalogue record for this book is available from
the British Library

ISBN 978-1-4739-1250-2
ISBN 978-1-4739-1251-9 (pbk)

Contents

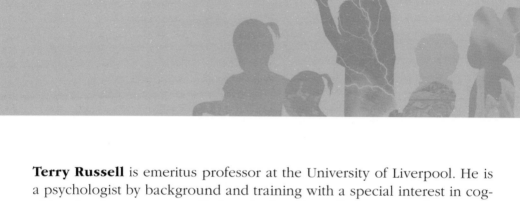

Author biographies

Terry Russell is emeritus professor at the University of Liverpool. He is a psychologist by background and training with a special interest in cognitive development as applied to the learning of science at all ages, but especially the younger age range. He taught in primary and secondary special needs schools and worked as an educational psychologist before finding opportunities to move into research. He has worked in South-East Asia, Africa and in the UK at King's College, London, and directed the Centre for Research in Primary Science and Technology at the University of Liverpool for over 20 years. He has directed national and international projects and published extensively. This book reflects his commitment to evidence-based activity that improves teachers' and pupils' educational experiences, where theory informs practice through practical and accessible applications.

Dr Linda McGuigan has an established record of research into the emergence and development of science understanding in the early years. Formerly a primary teacher and Deputy Director of the Centre for Research in Primary Science and Technology at the University of Liverpool, Linda has conducted and managed research into children's conceptual development in science, assessment and curriculum development. Attracting national and international interest, her work has been funded by national assessment and curriculum agencies. She has co-authored a number of books, reports, articles and digital and hard copy materials to support early years practice. Focusing on children's conceptual progression, she brings a developmental perspective to science learning, teaching and assessment. Linda's PhD investigated the impact of multimodal approaches on children's science learning. Multimodal learning continues to be an important feature of her research and professional development activities.

Acknowledgements

We are extremely grateful for the many ways in which children, staff and parents have supported our research over many years. Without their permission and goodwill our understanding could not have been furthered. We also thank the reviewers who kindly offered comment on our earlier drafts and staff at SAGE who helped us to realise the completion of this book.

How to use this book

There are a number of recurring features used within this book and this brief introduction indicates what they are and how to make use of them.

Chapter overviews

Each chapter uses a brief overview to set out the ground to be covered and acts as an 'advance organiser'.

Pauses for thought

Throughout, the book highlights illustrations of practice by drawing on real examples. Usually, these asides illustrate or elaborate best practice, as well as occasionally clarifying theoretical ideas. You might consider pausing as you read, and in your mind's eye, put yourself into the position of replicating some of the activities described in your own setting.

Reflections

The invitations to reflect are more direct than the 'Pauses for thought'. Occasionally, you might find them challenging. They are not onerous and you may find it useful to use them as discussion points with a colleague or in small groups as well as individually. The invitations to reflect are intended to promote the kind of thinking that will make it easier for you to engage with the text. The more effort you put into these reflections, the more you will benefit from them.

Background science

The background science pieces are nowhere near exhaustive either in coverage or in the detail of what is presented. They are included from time to time, where relevant, as a reminder that there is always some higher level science knowledge behind the text. Within the book the view is expressed explicitly that knowing some science is of benefit to educators of young children. It is well-established that many or most educators of young children lack confidence in their science knowledge background. 'Background science' is written with adults in mind and provides what we hope will be the starting point for adults to develop their own understanding. It is most certainly not intended or suited for transmission directly to children. These asides are intended to be apt and illustrative, perhaps intriguing, but certainly not exhaustive. Being better informed will help you to be aware of productive directions for questioning and exploratory activities that will be fruitful for children to pursue. We encourage you to take the time to explore science subject matter that you are not familiar with as it arises or ahead of a topic you intend to teach so that you understand it a little better. Our suggestion is that you should be at least as curious to know more as are the children in your care.

Chapter summaries

Each chapter ends with a bulleted summary of the main points discussed as a digest of the main features of the chapter and to help you to recap what you have read. These summaries are not intended to stand-alone: the substance is in each chapter.

Appendix: science activities and subject matter referred to in this book

We appreciate that educators of younger children often seek support for decisions about the science subject matter that children should be learning about and how to assess it when they wander 'off piste'. Throughout the book's chapters there is advice (both explicit and implicit via the examples discussed, some very fleetingly) about what might be taught and how to assess it. In the Appendix, we summarise the content mentioned throughout the pages as well as providing a succinct summary of how to assess any and every subject matter that might be touched upon. This Appendix is therefore not constrained by any curricular regime. It is applicable to curricula anywhere in the world and describes a procedure that is transferable to any age group.

Introduction

Chapter overview

This chapter introduces the foundational ideas for what is presented in subsequent chapters. Throughout the book, the authors emphasise the developmental journey that children take as they progress towards scientific understanding and how adults might nurture and support children along the route. The chapter describes the authors' approach to science in the early years and the evidence for the theoretical orientation adopted towards children's science learning.

What this book offers

Both authors have taught and researched extensively with teachers and practitioners working with the age range that is the interest of this book. We also bring a background in developmental psychology to established careers in applied educational research. We emphasise the practical application of research evidence to inform practice in settings and classrooms. The activities and the practical implementation of theory that we discuss are almost entirely tested through our own collaborative, classroom-based research with educators of young children. Our research orientation has been complemented by the classroom expertise of those working directly with children. This has been to mutual professional benefit as well as to the benefit of learners. We are interested in research that deals with the fundamental issues that help to make teaching and children's learning more effective, enjoyable and professionally informed. We wish to share our attitude of asking questions when in doubt, so as to inform thoughtful actions rather than to imagine we know all the answers that would allow us to suggest a set of off-the-shelf formulae. Research is as much about thinking analytically and asking ourselves questions about why things happen the way they do as it is about providing answers. This attitude of curiosity as to how we might improve outcomes for children is what we wish to convey to our fellow professionals.

Who is the book for?

The upper end of the age group with which this book is concerned will be 5–7 year olds subject to the Key Stage 1 (KS1) national curriculum, while the 3–5 age group will be subject to the Early Years Foundation Stage (EYFS) in England. The book is aimed at those adults who are responsible for the science learning of children in the 3–7 age range, whether in the private, voluntary or independent (PVI) sectors or in schools. It should be of interest to practitioners, teachers, students, classroom assistants and interested parents. We use the term 'educators' as it is sufficiently non-specific to cater for all those who have children in their care and teach young children without specifying their professional background and qualifications. We avoid the repeated use of 'practitioners in settings and teachers in schools', but may occasionally use one or other of the terms in the understanding that the message is intended for all those who support the young children who are the subject of this book. We take the view that, however formal or unstructured the ambience of the environment children attend, whatever the premises, the curriculum to which they are exposed or the professional background of those adults who supervise them, chil-dren have to be managed with care, insight and expertise. This book intends to contribute to the establishment and consolidation of those nec-essary conditions of professionalism. We are sympathetic to progress towards parity of esteem and equality of professional status between early years practitioners and the teachers (DfE, 2012, 2013a) who oversee children's educational needs across the 3–7 age range. Achievement of this goal will ensure that all young children receive the highest possible quality in the standard of professional care and support.

Only a small minority of learners achieves the highest levels. Many encounter impediments, struggle, or fall by the wayside for a variety of social or personal reasons. A family's socio-economic status ('social class') offers a strong correlation with educational success. For example, the outcomes of a study of 19,000 5 year olds' language capabilities concluded that 40% of the boys eligible for free school meals ('fsm', used as an index of poverty) start school below the expected level of language skills. One-third of the girls eligible for fsm were below the expected language level at 5 years (Finnegan and Warren, 2015). Forecasting the educational needs and outcomes for a 3 year old at some point 15 or 20 years hence (perhaps three or four elections for a politician) is an inexact business. These circumstances might also contribute to what is seen as an inappropriate 'top down' approach, whereby the expectations that apply later in the system are applied by administrators earlier, pushed downwards in an attempt to raise standards or forestall the difficulties apparent in older children.

Although we argue for taking heed of an essential continuity in development, this must be with an appreciation of the qualitative changes that occur through childhood. How do we act positively to support children's well-being, resilience and development? We wish to encourage educators to have the confidence to pause and think, and not feel pressurised to come up with instant solutions to every doubt that arises; examine what is happening attentively; stand back and reflect; and teach considerately to support children's progress. We do not favour the regimes of non-interventionists looking on with benign adult expressions, where the 'little ones' are left to their own devices. Children can enjoy the action, conversations, sounds, excitement, challenges and engagement that science contexts offer. Such activities offer far more than keeping children occupied. They must be seen as meaningful as well as stimulating, inspiring wider aspects of development. Science engagement need not always be all action, though it offers welcome opportunities of that variety. There also needs to be time for quiet thinking, contemplation, conversation, thoughtful analysis and evaluation, both for children and their mentors. We would like teachers to be alert to the potential of novelty in the routine, to keep teaching fresh and responsive. This is not easily accomplished, especially at the start of a career, but sharing uncertainties with children and colleagues should be seen as a better option than hiding doubt behind bravado. Teaching is an interactive pursuit, something done with children rather than to them. It requires flexibility and adaptability, informed by some sound guiding principles. We intend to set out those principles that underpin outstanding practice in nurturing science behaviours, attitudes and understanding. Be assured that these principles have sound cross-curricular relevance.

General and specific approaches to teaching science

Later in their educational journeys, learners will encounter science as a separate subject, a specialist area of the curriculum; in time, it will be taught by experts. At that later time, science will have its unique content – the subject matter particular to science, as well as its special processes – the ways of working, gathering information and using evidence. Adults who work with younger children have a wider responsibility for the whole child: social, emotional, physical, linguistic, moral and all aspects of cognitive, creative and imaginative development. Stated in those terms, taking responsibility for young children's educational development sounds like a hugely demanding responsibility. And of course, it is a serious business to be in charge of all these aspects of a child's growth.

Our argument is that a young child's science education has to be seen in that overall 'holistic' perspective – a rounded view of the needs of the whole child that is inclusive of growth in all areas, personal and curricular. Our interest in fostering ways of thinking about science does not seek to displace, steal time from or subordinate any other areas of the curriculum. Our aspiration is to complement advances in those other areas. It would be a mistake to pigeonhole science activities as concerned only with a special quality of thinking about specific subject matter, often caricatured as dispassionate, difficult, solitary and single-minded behaviour. Scientific activity also requires imaginative thinking, exchange of views, collaboration, curiosity, enthusiasm, creativity and drive. For younger children, it is often more helpful to think of 'science contexts', rather than 'doing science'. Science can emerge from broader, possibly familiar, situations within which some science content is relevant and perhaps significant without being isolated or decontextualised. Thinking of science subject matter in this broader cross-curricular fashion will make it easier to tie in almost any other subject matter or activity, not least stories. In fact, much of very engaging science experience begins with a fictional narrative from which the science content can readily emerge or be teased out, given a pinch of lateral thinking.

Age range and children's science capabilities

Childminders, nursery, pre-school, Reception and KS1 classes: these various contexts in which young children are looked after, nurtured, protected and educated all contribute to the development of children's thinking. Can we or should we try to partition when the 'early years' begin and when they end? The steps that children take in their transition from one organisation to another may be hugely significant to them as exciting, perhaps challenging, landmarks in their growth. Each also has its own set of rules, expectations, responsibilities, modes of operating and legal constraints, as well as being governed by curricular requirements or expectations. The value position that assumes the uniqueness of every child should permeate all these environments.

The normal distribution curve – the bell shaped graph that emerges when human physical and mental attributes are plotted against proportions of the population – confirms the spread of variation in many attributes, physical, cognitive and emotional. At each tail end of the curve, there will be a smaller proportion of cases than towards the middle, with the centre recording the most frequent, most commonly occurring incidence of the feature being observed. Such distributions confirm differences in development between children at any point in time: in physical prowess, language, social and self-confidence as well as interests in different subject matter. Children also differ widely in their interests and capabilities in reading, number and knowledge of the world. Yet there is also continuity in the steps, phases or progressions that children move through. Some may be ahead of the norm, others delayed; some may be late starters, others subject to spurts in growth, physical or mental or both.

We take the view that all educational needs, science included, require analysis and attention using the critically important tool of formative assessment. Formative assessment is the strategy of collecting evidence continuously for the purpose of informing action. It will be discussed in more detail in Chapter 8, 'Planning, assessment and recording keeping', but we recommend that the formative approach should permeate every aspect of working with children. This means that, as far as is reasonably manageable, individual children's needs must be identified rather than assumed on the basis of 'what most children need' or the norm for any particular group. Formative assessment provides the information that allows adults to distinguish between the different qualities of children's performance and helps them to respond in actions that are sensitive to the unique needs of each child. For this reason, we do not, in this book, have a separate section or way of thinking about 'special or additional educational needs'. We assume that children progress once their requirements have been identified and judicious support tailored to needs and achievements is provided. This applies to all children. It is a stance that avoids self-fulfilling prophecies associated with identifying certain individuals as 'behind' or 'delayed' (or whatever euphemism might be used). Once we establish where children are and what their next accomplishments should be, we must take the necessary steps to support their progress. So formative assessment also requires thinking ahead, with some anticipation of progressive steps in development. Treating each child's needs as unique is not such a tall order when the adult has an overview or some form of guideline to refer to of the journey that lies ahead.

Reflection

Normal distribution curves

All the curves in the diagram have the shape of a normal distribution, with frequencies tapering each side of the norm. Many human attributes are normally distributed: height, for example, with the most frequent height in the centre, shorter people to the left and taller people to the right. The extent to which any particular feature shows a spread of measurement varies.

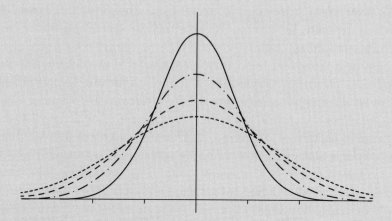

Figure 1.1   Normal distribution curves

Describe what you consider to be evidence of science capabilities in young children. Is science an area in which you expect a large spread of capability, or a more compressed curve, where performance tends to be fairly uniform? What sorts of science behaviours characterise children at the left and right hand extremes of the distribution?

Many people with responsibility for younger children feel a pressure to attain 'the basics'. They may also feel this expectation to be an unwelcome and mistaken intrusion on early childhood. Acquisition of the basics may be assumed to require structured and systematic teaching, perhaps with children sitting at a table rather than operating informally. The arguments against such teacher driven directed practices often refer to 'readiness', so we need to ask, 'readiness for what, exactly?'. Formal, directed instruction requires children to: sit still for a required period; pay attention; concentrate on the task in hand; and follow instructions. Most, if not all, children entering pre-school are not ready to comply with those conditions. They are growing very rapidly and learning to use the changing strength, agility and co-ordination of their bodies to explore their world. These are not trivial accomplishments, but are believed to influence both the development of muscle fibre and the establishment of new pathways in the brain known as 'cerebellar synaptogenesis' (Byers and Walker, 1995). Many species of mammals display this form of excessive and 'non-functional' motor activity as a critical period, a phase that occurs just once and is highly significant for development. (Think of the imprinting of ducks on the first moving object they encounter as an example of a critical period and the gambolling of lambs as a form of non-functional motor 'play'.) The exuberant energy of children may have longer-term adaptive value underpinning psychomotor intelligence, with direct implications for thinking capabilities. Shayer and colleagues (Shayer et al., 2007) compared performance on a science-related task concerned with ideas about volume and heaviness (capabilities directly related to concrete experiences of handling materials) between 1975 and 2003, and identified a decline in performance in children leaving primary school. While the design of the reported study makes the findings entirely credible, the causes behind significant decline in performance can only be speculative. However, an obvious candidate would be a parallel decline in direct experiences of handling real materials. This might in turn be associated with changes in lifestyles in which a more sedentary, possibly more computer-based forms of play are more prevalent in young children.

Inhelder and Piaget's (1958, 1964) notion of the development of intelligence as similar to an organism's physical adaptation to its environment is helpful in understanding the development of scientific thinking. They describe intellectual development as involving two processes through which humans adapt to the physical world. These two cognitive processes are assimilation and accommodation. Assimilation involves responding to, taking in and internalising experiences from the physical world; accommodation is the internal mental process whereby these new experiences are reconciled with what is already known. This hypothesis or model of what is happening in the mind-brain describes an organisation in the form of mental structures. Incidentally, many cognitive psychologists favour the term 'mind-brain' over either one or the other of 'mind' or 'brain' by itself. This is because the term 'mind-brain' treats mental activity as something within the structure and function of the physical organ. Furthermore, that physical organ is one component within a hominid body that has adapted through evolutionary processes to the physical environment of our world over millions of years. Although Inhelder and Piaget's formal stage-developmental theory (that is, the developmental shift through pre-operational to concrete and then formal operational thinking structures) has been criticised and undermined in some ways (for example, by followers' over-zealous inference of age norms) it retains its adherents and its association with productive research. The essential idea of intellectual growth as making sense of new experiences with what is already known remains a powerful insight to bring to the learning of science. This cognitive balancing between new and old, current and former experiences is a constantly ongoing and recurring adaptive process to establish a new equilibrium (through 'equilibration', as it is called). This is a lifelong process of enhancing understanding of the world by active minds.

Pause for thought

Emergent science

The expression of science ideas may be 'emergent' rather than fully formed, but will nonetheless offer a rich source of insight into a child's thinking for those adults determined to engage. The drawing in Figure 1.2, with written annotations and numbers, depicts a 5 year old's record of the outcome of a Formula One motor race. The rooftop speakers declaim the result. With a little decoding of the typical reversals of numbers and letters, we can discern the context and outcome: 'And the winner is (car number) 800. And the second was (car number) 75'.

Figure 1.2 provides opportunities for dialogue and questioning with its creator: 'What is that contraption on the left? Are those the overhead fuel pipes, or the airlines for fixing the wheels? (Good observation of detail!) Why do cars need fuel? What fuel do racing cars use? Is it

Figure 1.2   The value of being alert to emergent science ideas

the same as for family cars or buses? Why don't the racing cars fill up with enough to avoid stopping? Why do they change the tyres? It seems like they waste time! What was it about car 800 that allowed it to finish ahead of number 75? Which of our toy cars is the fastest? How could we find out? They don't use petrol, so how do they move? Why do they stop? How do words travel through the air as sound in different directions, yet the message still comes through in the correct order?' (The reversals in letter, number and word formation convey the conundrum, albeit fortuitously.)

This approach is one of asking and listening, not telling; conveying a sense of interest and curiosity; beginning with the child's starting point, not the adult's. The drawing, writing and numbers are strong steps in

(Continued)

(Continued)

the acquisition of 'the basics' as well as 'emergent science'. This starting point is a gift to a science educator and an illustration of how a 'bottom up' approach differs from 'top down' directed activity. It is child-initiated, but becomes more than child-centred when the adult takes the opportunity to subtly shape the raw enthusiasm towards the agenda of projected educational gains.

There is concern amongst some educators that pressure from 'above' may undermine the early years ethos and philosophy by emphasising formal outcomes attained through structured activities directed by adults, rather than child-centred processes. This concern might apply to any subject matter. Apprehensions about too great a formality can apply across the curriculum. We must be clear about the kind of scientific behaviour we have in mind as appropriate to the early years and be explicit that it is far from formal and much more about an attitude of mind and characteristic ways of thinking. Science in the early years doesn't need to resemble the stereotype of science in the public imagination. The iconic laboratories, test tubes, microscopes, and electrical components can wait their turn. For the early years, we emphasise ways of being curious about encounters in everyday contexts. The teachers who express a lack of confidence in their own science backgrounds can reassure themselves by calling on an enthusiasm to share in children's curiosity. They can draw on their cross-curricular expertise to model asking questions, devising simple enquiries, encouraging discussion and speculation. They can insist on requiring reasons and evidence for all expressed views. Science knowledge throughout the early years and beyond is necessarily provisional. Children's understanding will be approximate, always subject to later revision and refinement. The greatest scientific experts are likely to be the most modest in their claims and the most aware of how much more there remains to find out. Early years teachers can arouse and value curiosity and a questioning attitude as a constant state of mind in the children they influence. The processes of seeking answers and requiring evidence to support a point of view can complement this outlook. Sharing such a world view and set of values about 'finding out' and the desire to understand more has the power to ignite a lifelong and unquenchable flame. The interesting and perhaps surprising conclusion is that the scientific attitudes described here can be applied to just about every aspect of life and learning, not just science, and to both teachers and children.

Combatting inequality

It is a fact that children from underprivileged groups are under-represented at the highest levels of educational achievement and at the highest levels of office in public life (Goodman and Gregg, 2010). Of course, some children from disadvantaged backgrounds will be found among those who flourish. At 22 months, children who have low cognitive scores but who grow up in families of high socio-economic position have been found to improve their relative scores as they approach the age of 10 years. The relative position of children with high scores at 22 months, but who grow up in families of low socio-economic position, worsens as they approach 10 years (Marmot, 2010). A follow-up study (Marmot, 2014) found that, on average, levels of development at 5 years were worse for all children in deprived areas. The study reported just over half (52%) of all children in England achieved a 'good' level of development at 5 years whereas only about a third (36%) of children eligible for fsm achieved that level at the same age. These outcomes must be of concern to policy makers. Think of a wedge between the higher and the lower achievers in the ascending line of achievement over time. The angle of that wedge gets steeper with increasing age, the gap greater. This is the disadvantage educators are trying to reduce. We have to value our young children, both to realise the prospects of their individual blossoming and from the perspective of the social resource they represent. What does this mean in practice? The development of communicative skills is a ubiquitous priority for early years professionals. It requires giving children opportunities to experience a rich language environment, to develop their confidence and skills in expressing themselves, and to speak and listen in a range of situations. Our position with respect to language and science is not the reminder that, 'Oh, by the way, science offers children opportunities to encounter new vocabulary'. Our claim is deeper and more far-reaching. All areas of the curriculum offer potential for language development. Science activities are much more than incidental in this regard. Science calls on listening carefully to others' arguments, thinking, reflecting, reasoning and expressing oneself lucidly with precise (occasionally specialist) vocabulary. These are reasons enough to counter any protestations of 'must attend to the basics – not enough time' to include science.

Appreciating how children develop science understanding

Throughout this book we will refer to some fundamental assumptions about how learning in science happens. As we review these processes, we will consider how such learning may be facilitated. We apply our theory to our own writing and recommend all educators adopt this reflexive attitude: make sure your theories are applied to your own thinking and learning, as well as to children in your care. The fundamental and recurring question must be, 'What is the evidence for this belief or assertion?'. Science requires evidence for claims, and in a similar manner, we should require children to provide a backing for their ideas or assertions. We can gain insights into how this can be encouraged by observing children's learning in action and to some extent, by introspection on the processes of our own learning.

In order to support the development of children's science knowledge and skills, professionals need to have a guiding theory. While our driving mission is practical, applied, down-to-earth action to support children's development, we have no hesitation in championing the benefits of applying theoretical insights. There is a diverse range of theories of learning underpinned by different disciplines. We choose between theories by examining evidence about the practical benefits for action and positive learning outcomes. We buy into a theory for its payoff, its heuristic value: where its insights lead us, the new perspectives it opens up and new ways of dealing with challenges. A theory provides us with guidelines for practical decision making and action. Foundational ideas enable a conscious dialogue to take place in our heads, an inner conversation supported by key reference points. Our reflections then empower us to make informed decisions guided by explicit principles. We draw upon and bring to your attention evidence and insights from an area referred to as 'neuroconstructivist'. This recent and growing area attempts to bring together perspectives on teaching processes, cognition, brain activity, genetics and environmental factors to understand learning processes better (Westermann et al., 2010).

The 'representation of knowledge', 'multimodality' and 'metacognition'

We will now introduce and define a few terms that we use recurrently. The definitions are of ideas that have very practical consequences for interactions with learners (of all ages, actually). The principles, once grasped and internalised, can be applied again and again to support meaningful learning.

The word 'representation' is important to us when we speak about ideas and we use it frequently, with good reason. It is a word that we find sets us on the right direction in response to the question, 'How do children's experiences of the physical, "outside" world become familiar as the science knowledge inside their heads?'. We carry those learnings around with us and refer to them in the absence of the physical objects to which they refer by storing experiences as memories in our mind-brains. Without a memory, we would live in a constant present in which nothing was familiar and everything would be unpredictable (Sacks, 1985). Before considering how we form science concepts such as 'solid', 'liquid', 'animal', we can ponder an everyday concept familiar to most of us: a 'Mum'. We know her physically, in a form that is *presented* to us materially; in the absence of her physical presence, we have a *re-presentation* we carry around with us in memory. We have a concept of 'Mum-ness', a more general idea, rather like a 3-D spider diagram reaching through to the different parts of our brains handling different modes of information. In this internalised representation, a whole range of qualities – appearance, sound of voice, touch, emotional response and many other attributes – are all linked. Furthermore, our construction of Mum-ness also gives rise to expectations, like prototypes, to which we expect experiences to conform. So we are thinking of a 'representation' as a set of attributes that defines an idea or concept in the absence of its physical presence. The representation is portable: we carry the notion around with us in its physical absence, generalise from it to similar circumstances and refer to it to make predictions about how we expect things will turn out.

Recent study into the development of the brain allows neuroscientists to wire people up in a non-intrusive way (no surgery required) as they engage in thinking tasks. It has been known for some time that different areas of the brain are the sites of different faculties or capabilities. We know the brain comprises two hemispheres – left and right – one side being dominant, so that in right-handed people, the left hemisphere controls physical or 'motor' activity, while language behaviour is located on the right side. This fairly blunt information has been gained from findings from neuro-psychological patients having specific deficits, the unhappy outcomes of accidents, strokes, war injuries and other trauma. Current technology is much sharper and as individuals process particular ideas, electronic devices are able to reveal centres of activity caused by the firing of brain cells. One fascinating revelation is that several different locations within the brain are likely to 'light up' in association with even a relatively simple idea. Scanning their brain while a person focuses on a particular idea reveals a pattern of pathways, like tendrils to particular locations that are known to be associated with certain functions. Neuroscientists speculate that, in the future, it will be possible to scan for the ideas going on inside people's heads.

Science journalists who report this area of work, admittedly heading in the direction of science fiction, suggest that airport scanners will be developed to discern not only what we are carrying inside and outside our bodies, but also something of what we are thinking.

A representation would appear to have a complex physical correlate with a pattern of firing neurons in the mind-brain. The common rough estimate is of 100 billion neurons in the human brain, interconnected by 150 trillion links or 'synapses'. The simple fact to hold on to is that the scope for complexity is enormous. We are some considerable way off neurologists being able to tell us in real time how children's science ideas are progressing. Nonetheless, the idea we will pursue here is that science concepts can be thought of as representations held in progressively specialised linked areas or 'modules' of the mind-brain. Modules (units or components) have some particular functional relationship with the physical world. It will be worth the effort to think a little more deeply about modes of thinking and behaving and multimodality in science learning. There are real implications for practice.

Modularity and embodied cognition

In the 1980s, cognitive science suggested (Fodor, 1983) that some mental or cognitive processes are structured as 'modules'. These are relatively separate and fast-acting sub-routines in cognitive activity. Modules can be defined as mind-brain mechanisms for transforming environmental stimuli into a human-usable form. More recently, some cognitive psychologists have explored the idea of 'embodied cognition' (Wilson, 2008), reacting against the idea of the brain as an organ that works on its own and that deals only with abstractions, like the remote executive of a company. The reality is that the brain is part of the body that has adapted to survival in a physical environment over evolutionary time. It works in combination with our physical movements, intentions, emotions and neural processes. Because the ways of receiving information from the world (seeing, hearing, touching, etc.) are so familiar to us, we need to stand back and think of ourselves (as if from an alien's perspective) as physical systems in a physical world. We are immersed in various forms of energy that impact on us: light waves, sound vibrations and forces of various kinds. There is no single way in which organisms in the animal kingdom recognise and organise these input stimuli. Male whales 'sing', their songs conducted over immense distances through water, to let females know they are interested. Dolphins click and bats emit high-pitched squeaks to locate objects in their vicinity (echolocation) and to communicate. Elephants make very low frequency rumbles with their stomachs.

Humans cannot interpret all the signals used by other animals, but the *modes* – generating and receiving sound and using light energy for vision – are familiar to us. Human nervous systems are somehow organised into *modules* to receive these stimuli as a first step and then, step two, to organise them into the right area of the brain to use them to register and maybe modify responses to the world. Most *modular* responsiveness is automatic and lightning quick. We flinch at a loud noise, recoil from fast moving objects, salivate and move towards appetising smells. It is the relative independence and autonomy of these neural circuits that are brought into play without conscious reflection that suggests *modularity*, or the relative separateness of the units involved. It seems that conscious awareness of these various inputs happens only at a third level of cognitive organisation, where we think about inputs. Most of the animal kingdom survives perfectly well without this third, conscious level of operating (though there are scientists who suggest that some animals – whales and dolphins for example – have consciousness). Humans are different. We evaluate what is going on in a self-aware manner, making sense of the myriad impressions that impinge upon us. (It takes effort and uses energy, so we switch off or 'turn off' from time to time.) The conscious overviewing job, like the functioning of an airport control tower, has to some extent a control and command function. It is a capability that is correlated with the development of the greatly enlarged frontal cortex in the modern human brain as compared with our hominid ancestors. Much of education is concerned about working in this area of conscious reflection on experience, often referred to as 'metacognition' or thinking about our own thought processes.

Pause for thought

Multimodal representations

Each of us constructs ideas inside the mind-brain about things we encounter. We carry around the objects and events the world presents to us as ideas or 're-presentations'. This means that we know about them and can think about them even in their absence. Representations can be constructed through several different modes – through the senses and through other modes of knowing and imagery, including speech and text. Much learning can take place independent of language or prior to the words being available to describe the experience.

(Continued)

(Continued)

The photographic image is itself a visual representation with written annotations to show some of the ways that a child can come to know about an apple. These modes include using sight, taste, hearing, touch and language. Understanding continues to grow – of different varieties of apples, their dietary value – even recreational use of the fact that apples float and can be used in party games. Later in primary school, feeling the force of gravity acting on a typical apple's mass of about 100g held on the flat palm of the hand is a useful way of representing the unit of force that is one newton.

Figure 1.3   A child's multimodal representations of an apple

A theory of cognitive functioning as involving different modalities may seem complex, but makes sense in the light of our everyday experience of the sense *modalities* that we will discuss in the context of young children learning science. Our senses and their receptors are usually described as including vision (using the eyes); hearing (ears); touch, along with temperature sensitivity (via the skin); taste (tongue) and the closely related sense of smell (nose). A sense of balance and the orientation of the body in space are achieved via receptors in the inner ear. Sense modalities and cognitive modules are not the same thing, but have features in common that support our ideas about how the theory of modularity can be of practical use to educators. How the senses work and how they are linked neurally to particular areas of the brain is a helpful way of introducing localisation and specificity of function. But there are more cognitive modules posited than the five or six senses. For example, some psycholinguists consider language to be a module, though others disagree, pointing to maturation as the determining factor. There is controversy over whether language is a ready-made, pre-formed and hard-wired module in the brain available to infants (Chomsky, 2006; Pinker, 2013). (The alternative theory is that language is a facility that is learned and that develops through experience and maturation.) Face and voice recognition is more generally thought of as a module; think how many unique familiar faces or voices we instantly recognise in a crowd (even if recalling names lags behind). This instantaneous processing is the sort of evidence that argues for the presence of modules. The theory is interesting and has clear application: we just need to exercise some caution. The degree to which the development of modules is susceptible to environmental influence is the subject of current research.

Modules and development

As suggested above, one way of thinking about modules is as something we are born with, a 'nativist' assumption about hard-wiring from birth. In an important challenge to and elaboration of this formulation, it has been suggested that modularisation is better understood as a developmental process (Karmiloff-Smith, 2012). For this to be the case, it has to be assumed that modules are plastic or malleable, shaped by the course of development rather than determined by genes alone and fixed at birth (Russell, 2015a). Arguments for the developmental plasticity of the infant brain refer to the evidence of localised differences in the density of brain cells in the newborn brain, or the different thresholds at which they fire. It is thought that different brain regions compete for processing priority. Over time, as the result of particular interactions with the environment, the 'domain relevant' areas develop into 'domain specific' regions, specialising in processing particular kinds of information. For instance, children's very early skill in recognising familiar faces might be understood as the fine-tuning of an initial 'domain relevant' capability to recognise visual patterns more generally, rather than human faces specifically. Learning and development is thus understood to be a process that involves mutually influencing interactions between the brain, environment, genes and behaviour. This is a new and important area of scientific investigation: 'epigenetics' (Carey, 2012).

Modularisation suggests that certain ways of thinking are likely to become predominant in an individual's thinking, something like 'mainline' routes through which cognitive processing will operate faster and become more automatic. If we think of lifestyles and learning over historical timescales, we can appreciate that some modes of thinking that have become habitual in modern societies are likely to have been very different in former times. Literacy is no longer the preserve of the aristocracy. Almost every aspect of modern life is quantified using standardised scales of measurement. From the late twentieth century to the present, the developed world has been subject to a revolution in access to digital information and communications. This exposure is happening at an increasingly younger age and the argument about plasticity in the development of brain function suggests that these changes impact on the structure of the mind-brain and way we think (Shayer et al., 2007). Artificial light and heat blur our awareness of night and day and the seasons. Urban dwellers lack the possibility of seeing the stars because of our light-polluted environment – the very source of mystery that fed early scientific curiosity about our place in the universe. More positively, twenty-first century learners have access to an enormous range of multimedia digital representations, unparalleled in earlier generations. This scale of resource is available to science educators to use to represent ideas that would have been inaccessible to earlier generations. Concepts that might be rarely occurring, dangerous or at the extremes of scale have become accessible. It does not seem reasonable to limit children's access to only that which they can see and touch as interpreters of Piaget once advocated, when digital animations and images available to children today include wonders such as a photograph of a single atom.

Any single representation can only ever approximate to some attributes of the thing that is represented. For example, a photographic image of a frog will very successfully convey a view from one perspective; scale can be indicated, colour also, but not temperature or sound. Karmiloff-Smith (1995) has elaborated the role of conscious awareness as we translate between representations in a process she calls 'representational redescription' (or 'RR'). RR attempts to describe how we consciously move between one representational modality and another. This is a metacognitive process (that is, it requires thinking about our own thinking) to generate transformations that enrich our conceptual understanding. Metacognition is important in meaningful learning: generative meaning-creating behaviour requires reflective brainwork. The phenomenological experience – that which we are aware of through introspection – is often one of mental struggle to make the transformation explicit. The process requires effort and concentration.

We often see this struggle in children's screwed up faces and agitated wriggling as they tussle (with that third level conscious function) to express their ideas. As adults, a similar struggle is invoked when an idea needs a word in order to find expression – one that is 'on the tip of the tongue', but has to be dragged from the subliminal to conscious awareness. The meaning has to be 'nailed' to be made explicit. These explicitations can be articulated externally (rather than internally, as thoughts) to be fully realised. These expressions (or representations) may take the form of diagrams, speech, writing, or some other format. Consciously moving between representations using different modalities facilitates sense making by triangulating modes, producing the sense of a more secure understanding. This theoretical perspective opens up a dynamic way of thinking about learning as actively transformative rather than passively receptive. The applications to science learning will be discussed in more detail in later chapters.

Our formulation of a productive approach draws on various sources of current neuroconstructivist theory while acknowledging that this is a discipline still in relative infancy. In adopting a constructivist approach towards learning and teaching, we are guided by these advances. There are immediate practical implications that can be derived for early years practice as a whole and for supporting early science thinking in particular. It is of interest that while our reformulation leads to a particular set of recommendations, the advocacy is not greatly at odds with practices such as those arrived at through more intuitive professional practices under various early years banners. For example, although we do not specify any particular number in the range of representational formats available to the 3–7 age group, we are comfortable with the promotion of ideas such as Reggio Emilia's 'hundred languages of children' (Edwards and Gandini, 2011). The role of direct experience is widely held to be critically important to children's early education and our formulation shares that value while drawing our own implications for practice.

Reflection

How would you summarise our approach to early years education as authors of this book? Consider whether there are some ideas that you are going to need more time, discussion, further reading and reflection in order to grasp fully.

Pause for thought

Multimodal experience

As children explored the garden adjacent to their room, an adult spotted a frog in the undergrowth. (The frog had been seen previously and anticipated by pictures and reference books being provided, close at hand.) She called to the children, 'Quick, look a frog. Where is it? Can you see?'. She anticipated that observations of the frog would provide opportunity for language development. Children gathered around and looked eagerly for the frog. The adult asked, 'What does it look like? Is it the same frog we've seen before? Where do you think it lives? The practitioner's questions encouraged children to look carefully at the frog's eyes, and legs and colour. They offered short verbal observations: 'It's brown'; 'Its throat is moving'. They jumped themselves, as the frog jumped, like a frog, feet together, from a crouched position. A child made noises, soon joined by others: 'riggit', 'riggit'. The frog was held briefly and very carefully, the children examining it through a hand lens, before releasing it back into the foliage. Some children looked at the pictures of frogs while others made drawings. Some were encouraged to make 3-D models, comparing their artworks with photographs and pictures in books and finding out more about frogs using the internet.

Children's responses used several sense modalities (though not smell or taste in this instance). They observed carefully, touched the frog. They verbalised their experiences, looked at images, possibly read and wrote a few words, drew pictures and made models. They used whole body movements and gestures. They might later be asked to consider the swimming action used by frogs and compare it with their own styles. 'Which swimming style is closer to the one frogs use, front crawl or breaststroke?' Any single aspect of the experience would allow a child to construct a limited, one-dimensional internal representation of 'frog-ness'. Together, the attributes built up to a rounded sense of what a frog is, with further scope for thinking about its environment and place in the world, alongside other animals and plants.

Summary

The basic ideas and assumptions that shape the authors' thinking have been set out and will be developed in subsequent chapters.

- The encouragement of imagination, creativity and curiosity are the bedrock of scientific thinking. While independent thinking is valued, so also are collaboration, the expression and exchange of ideas and reflection.
- A gradual shift from holistic and child-led experiences towards increasingly adult-influenced (often science-specific) experiences is an acknowledged feature of early years provision. Our view is that the educator's role must always be active and engaged with children's thinking, whatever or whoever motivated an activity originally.
- Adults' questioning conversations and attentive responses nurture children's developing confidence to express and explore their ideas further.
- Our advocation of multimodal thinking and a full range of representational capacities resonate with many of the intuitive practices and underpinning principles of established early years educators.
- We refer to current neuroconstructivist theory and advocate an approach that promotes assumptions about the plasticity of young children's cognitive development. We are committed to the value of children's own transcriptions between representations expressed in different modes or formats.

2

The nature of early years science

Chapter overview

This chapter discusses the thinking and history behind science being introduced to children in primary and early years education, and some of the difficulties that practitioners and teachers encounter if they lack confidence in their science background. The authors' stance is to encourage working from existing professional strengths rather than to focus on deficits, including a consideration of using starting points such as narrative fiction. In the search for progression in the development of children's science thinking – also known as 'conceptual trajectories' – the skills that lay the foundations for scientific thinking are discussed.

Science education in the early years

Science as a subject alongside the 'three Rs' in the primary curriculum is a fairly recent, mid-twentieth century, phenomenon (Harlen, 2008), well after it had established its place in the secondary phase of education. It took a paradigm shift in educational thinking to recognise that young children's learning is in large part an active, self-directed activity. Enquiring young minds do not wait for adults to decide when they are ready to start making sense of their world. Sense making began to be seen as a biological necessity, a drive towards intellectual adaptation to the environment within the broader process of human evolution. This radical change in outlook displaced the passive, adult-driven process satirised in Dickens' *Hard Times* (1996) in which the schoolmaster Thomas Gradgrind's pedagogical style embraced only the cramming of facts. The emergence of cognitive developmental psychology as a discipline raised awareness of children's scientific and mathematical reasoning processes (Isaacs, 1962). Using a new framework to guide research ('genetic epistemology' or the developmental construction of knowledge) it was possible to describe, even from infancy, how intelligent behaviour emerges. This developmental perspective was informed by empirical investigations that included listening to children as they dealt with various logical or mathematical problems. This was a radical foray into what previously had been the territory of philosophers.

The exact nature of the science appropriate for young children was not an immediately settled matter. For a number of years, there has been debate about the precise qualities of science thinking behaviour to which we should aspire for children in primary education. From early in the introduction of science as a school subject, there has been a debate that has see-sawed back and forth: should we prioritise the 'what' (science concepts) or the 'how' (science processes) of science? The proponents of the 'what' side wished to lay the foundations for the big ideas that have shaped modern culture (evolution, the solar system, electricity, chemistry, energy, etc.), while the 'how' advocates favoured introducing children to science processes (the ways of experimental enquiry practiced by scientists). This fluctuating debate has matured into what is currently a more nuanced position.

The major guiding principles of science education

In more recent years, the process–concept dichotomy has become refined into a more elaborated structure and set of expectations (see, for example, Duschl et al., 2007, p. 36). There tend to be four major concerns that, though interacting, have separately identifiable features.

1. **Conceptual understanding**: the 'what' of science, knowing about the subject matter, the concepts or scientific ideas that are widely accepted and used by scientists to explain the natural world.
2. **Science processes**: the 'how' of science, to know about and engage in practical scientific enquiries as the principal mode for generating and putting to the test scientific evidence and explanations.

3. **The rules associated with the acceptance of science knowledge**: how science knowledge is unique and differs from other kinds of knowledge; how knowledge claims are made and supported, more formally stated as the 'epistemic nature of scientific knowledge'.
4. **The nature of science discourse**: how scientists arrive at agreed (provisional or disputed) understanding through talking, writing and doing science. This implies being aware of the 'rules of the game' of participation in scientific exchanges; knowing what counts as evidence and the acceptable ways of making and challenging claims.

With varying degrees of prominence, these principles guide the scope of science education, applying to a much wider age range than our focus on 3–7 year olds. While primary or elementary science has a minority stake in that larger enterprise and 'emergent science' an even smaller and more recent presence, the same guiding principles apply. The perspective adopted, as throughout this book, is that early years educators must look both to earlier and later events to establish firm foundations and a consistent trajectory. The challenge is to frame expectations in age-appropriate form. To this end, the narrative set out in this book elaborates the guiding principles in each of three chapters: Chapter 4 deals with conceptual development; Chapter 5 examines working scientifically; Chapter 6 discusses children engaging in scientific discourse by giving reasons for their ideas and increasing their capability to use evidence to support those ideas.

Science in the early years context

Science educators must be sensitive to the interface with the broader context and principles of early years education. That wider context assumes an important role for practitioners and teachers in partnership with parents in nurturing children's understanding, reasoning and science skills. Science is one area amongst the many that are important in every child's development. Early years education rightly adopts an integrated or holistic approach to the all-round development of every child. Providers and consumers expect high-quality learning, with demonstrable progress towards early learning goals, both within the fundamental underpinning capabilities and in specific areas of learning. Science, as with other specific areas of the curriculum, is expected to be encouraged within approaches that focus on the individual and foster positive relationships. The entire learning environment must be one that is enabling and acknowledges children's differing needs and rates of progress.

The expectations for science-related provision are introduced for the most part within the broad expectation that children should learn to understand the world and the objects and events that they are likely to encounter within it, either directly or indirectly. This is a broad agenda, but the lack of detailed specification allows local circumstances and special interests to have their place. In England, the major themes include people, communities, environment (including animals and plants) and materials – again, a very broad agenda. Other themes relevant to science can be discerned in every area of the curriculum, as we stress throughout this book, so our advice is, if you see a spark of interest, pursue it and fan it into flames.

Following their starting school (at approximately 5 years of age in the UK), children are expected to become increasingly ready to access the science-specific requirements of the curriculum. While most schools share some of the concerns of early years educators to develop the whole child, science can be expected to form a more discrete element of teachers' planning once children are attending school. But not all science activity needs to be planned. Allowance should be made for exciting but unplanned serendipity. The range of explorations and enquiries fostered within pre-school settings can be extended and modified to fit with the early demands of 'working scientifically'. Children's developing capabilities to express their ideas and to reason orally will enable interactions centred on ideas and evidence to flow more readily. Group interactions can give rise to exchanges of discourse that are recognisable as early forms of 'argumentation' (discussed in Chapter 6). Science developed in the pre-school will provide the foundation for children to construct new understandings. With children's overall development will arrive an increasing range of age-appropriate science topics.

Confidence and competence of educators

Although only a minority of people use science (or more broadly, science, technology, engineering and mathematics – 'STEM') directly in their income-generating occupations, it touches all of us in our daily lives. This impact reaches beyond consumer products and technical applications to ways of thinking, knowing, finding out, evaluating and discussing. These 'logico-scientific' behaviours are critically important not just for science education but because they impinge on many other subjects in the curriculum as they are encountered throughout lifelong learning. Little systematic evidence is available about the science backgrounds, qualifications and training of early years staff.

A review of childcare training (the 'Nutbrown Review', DfE, 2012) recommended minimum entry requirements and improvements in the criteria for early years qualifications. Insights into the professional development needs of early years teachers in relation to science (Copley and Padron, 1999) describe how early childhood educators view maths and science as difficult subjects, 'ones they felt unable to teach'. Increasing attention is being paid to the more general training and qualifications of early years professionals in England. New criteria for early years educator qualifications (DfE, 2013b) and new standards to be achieved by early years teachers (DfE, 2013c) aim to bring about more general improvements in the accomplishments of early childhood educators. Evidence of educators' confidence, qualifications and training in relation to science has tended to refer to teachers of the 5–11 age range. For example, Murphy and Beggs (2005) reported a lack of confidence and competence in the teaching of science in the primary phase of education, particularly physical science:

> Teachers felt that their overall lack of science background knowledge, confidence and training to teach science effectively was the most significant issue currently facing primary science. (Murphy and Beggs, 2005, p.7)

Harlen's (Holroyd and Harlen, 1996; Harlen, 1997) explorations through interviews with primary teachers in Scotland (n=55) reported how this group coped with a subject many found problematic. Teachers' reporting of defensive strategies remains particularly interesting and is likely to resonate with some educators today. Avoidance included teaching as little science as possible and eschewing practical work that might 'go wrong'. Physical science would be sidestepped, with more confidence shown in biological topics. Work cards offering step-by-step structure and exposition would be favoured as offering a handrail. Teachers saw emphasising a process approach as a positive coping strategy – that is, using science methods rather than addressing science subject matter content. As science educators, we can infer that the consequence would be a neglect of any deeper consideration of conceptual issues requiring science content understanding.

We can be sure that misgivings about the sufficiency of their own science knowledge still pertains amongst the educators of young children. Many adults who manage the science learning of young children are likely to be employing various coping or defending strategies to maintain their professional self-esteem. In the face of doubt, it seems entirely legitimate to utilise wider pedagogic skills when teaching science. The more general professional teaching techniques of planning, listening, questioning, evaluating and so forth apply to science as much as to any other subject. The thinking and reasoning skills that pervade the language and mathematics curricula have definite relevance to science learning. This survival strategy is not ideal, but does offer a first-aid sticking plaster, though it is important to appreciate the disadvantages. The benefit of educators' enhanced science background knowledge is not to enable the transmission of facts in a top-down fashion. Rather, conceptual science knowledge allows educators to use the insights available from their science understanding to interact with children more knowledgeably. It allows them to deploy pedagogical content knowledge or 'PCK' (Shulman, 1987). PCK requires knowing not just what science to teach but how and when to teach it. It confers an overview, a broader perspective, a map of any particular domain that includes the byways into which learners are likely to stray as well as the more direct routes to understanding. PCK will include knowledge of the experiences, resources and scaffolding techniques having proven effectiveness. Understanding the subject matter in greater depth will also enable more effective formative assessment judgements to be made.

Children's attitudes towards science

Attitudes and beliefs are complicated. Children's science attitudes can be thought of as a disposition towards learning and engaging in the subject; views about the impact of science on their own well-being and that of the planet; beliefs about the kinds of people that scientists are and how closely they might identify with them (and thus, their career choices); and beliefs about the nature of science (NoS) as a discipline. It is the first of these that is especially important and within the scope of early years experiences, where a positive attitude of mind towards science is going to be subject to the influence of the adults around children and the kinds of science activities they experience. Throughout education, science should be associated with curiosity and wonder about every aspect of the world. The subject should inculcate inquisitiveness and excitement about the unfamiliar while dispelling apprehension about the unknown. Science is about finding out. It offers myriad chances for exploring, for observing novel objects, materials and events. It is possible that children bring attitudes towards science along with them to their educational context, influenced by others, either positively or negatively. But the inspiration and imagination of teachers is a key factor in introducing creativity to science explorations and will influence children's outlook towards STEM subjects. Stylianidou and Agogi (2014), drawing on data from a study of creativity in early years science across nine countries, describe some of the teaching approaches associated with creativity in early years science as including planning motivating contexts linked to children's interests and physical exploration of materials.

Approaches including questioning and fostering curiosity were judged to be enabling of creativity. Frost (1997) emphasises the creativity entailed in teaching generally and in planning science experiences in particular. Planning means drawing together personal and professional experience, making imaginative use of available and relevant resources and co-ordinating everything within time constraints. As with any organised group activity, when science activities are productive, positive and pleasurable, the work put into planning is invisible.

Open-ended interactions tend to exploit children's interests, engage their attention and encourage persistence and curiosity. They are thus the bases for developing positive dispositions towards science learning. Fostering positive attitudes towards learning by engaging children's interest generally and science activities in particular has been found to be associated with their later achievement in science. In a longitudinal study following 4–8 year old children, Leibham et al. (2013) found that early science interests shaped the development of children's self-concept and influenced their later school science achievement. Interest in and attitudes towards science do not develop in isolation. The behaviours and values of the family and wider community can be expected to be influential. There is some evidence of children maintaining a long-term interest in science where parents have cultivated activity in science-related contexts in the home. Alexander et al. (2012) probed parental support for science learning at home in a longitudinal study and found sustained interest among children whose families created activities with contexts for science learning.

Holistic and subject-specific practices

Early years educators rightly think of their responsibilities as being to the whole child and their all-round needs, viewed within the framework of the whole curriculum. The implication is that pedagogical content knowledge relevant to the age range is closely linked to the theory and practice of child development. The teaching and learning agenda must always be mindful of the development of the whole child. Only gradually is subject-specific expertise a requirement and an advantage. It makes no sense to think of an 'on–off' switch tripped by administrative contingencies that compels teaching to abandon holistic concerns at a particular age or juncture in a child's education. The determining factor in any shift in practice must be considerations of children's development: are they performing at an average level, accelerating ahead or revealing evidence of developmental delay? The conceptual demands of science need to be introduced into the curriculum very gradually, from a broad, everyday context. In this light, less than completely assured subject-specific knowledge need not be detrimental. It will not be the cause of irreparable damage. On the other hand, educators having an enthusiasm for STEM subjects, as in any other area of the curriculum, are likely to be in a position to bring more dimensions and greater stimulation to their interactions with children.

The enormous complexity of science can be overwhelming to non-specialist educators. Being clear about the particular expectations for the early years group will introduce some reassuring realism. All educators should expect to grow in their chosen profession and this can happen alongside and through interacting with children. Science is a subject that feeds on curiosity and a desire to discover. This attitude can and should be a mutual experience between adults and children. The further children move through primary and into secondary education, the greater the need for specialist science conceptual knowledge becomes. In working with younger children and emergent science, the processes of thinking and behaving scientifically will be of pre-eminent concern rather than accumulating science factual knowledge. While we recommend a holistic approach as entirely appropriate for the needs of children in the lower end of the 3–7 age range, we intend to be very clear about what we mean by this. A statement to the effect, 'we cover science as it comes up in other subjects', without accompanying explicit objectives could be a self-deluding and defensive posture that lacks substance. Positive links with other subjects can and should be made, with advantages in both directions. Links with mathematics and literacy are easy to discern, but no less so also with history, geography, physical education, drama and art and design. For example, painting could touch upon the materials that can be painted on and different kinds of paint, sources of pigment, papermaking, colour mixing and light as well as how paintings change over time – colours fading, paper curling and becoming brittle. This 'Renaissance' attitude is closer to the impact of science in everyday life than the narrow boundaries defined by examination syllabi. Our advice to educators is to enjoy the freedom offered (albeit tacitly) by the early years (DfE, 2014) framework and the very broad latitude implied by the KS1 (DfE, 2013d) curriculum by offering children a broad and balanced science experience.

Stories and emergent science

Narrative fiction is a staple of early years education and one that may offer a starting point for science enquiries. We all love the sharing of other worlds that stories invite. They cost little, if anything, beyond some time and personalised attention that the favoured among us have experienced from our earliest awareness through bedtime stories. Active listening and participation in the action – dressing up, wearing masks or make-up, holding symbolic objects to fit the plot – seem to be adopted naturally by children. Involvement is contagious and like pantomime routines, draws on an intuitive sense that needs no drama school training. So it is that the early years scene of children closely packed on the carpet around the adult, attracted to the picture book like paper clips to a magnet, is a familiar one. The spell emanates from the narrative and images, enhanced by their artful deployment by the narrator to draw in children's involvement. Such a powerful device warrants a closer analysis for its science education potential.

In presenting stories of various kinds to non-readers (or those at the early stages of acquiring the skill), educators have at their disposal a technique that offers far more than entertainment or recreation. There is an enormous range of high-quality picture books and non-fictional expositions of science-relevant information available, accompanied by high-quality graphics. Adults can introduce these, or make them available to children. There are also biographies of eminent scientists, simplified to ensure accessibility. These widen children's awareness, broaden their geographical horizons and excite interest, respect and possibly personal ambition to be involved in STEM. In recent years, there have been efforts to redress the ethnic and gender imbalance that might have been orthodox in earlier times.

Some science educators acknowledge the possibilities of using a narrative form to communicate science to the public in a more meaningful and accessible manner (Avraamidou and Osborne, 2009). Norris et al. (2005) developed a framework for distinguishing narrative explanations from other kinds. They define eight elements that are present in a narrative:

1. events
2. change of state
3. narrative appetite (in the listener or reader)
4. passage of time
5. structure
6. agency
7. purpose, and
8. a listener or reader who is actively making meaning.

By closely defining narrative and the quality of explanation it supports, they suggest it should be possible to examine the claims made for narrative science explanations. They neither accept nor reject claims of 'improved memory for content, enhanced interest in learning, and greater comprehension of what is learned' (Norris et al., 2005, p. 552) and conclude:

> We are all *agents* with *purposes* of some sort whose lives inevitably consist of a series of *events* situated in *time*. This being the case, and these being the fundamental properties of narratives, it is not a large leap to the notion that the 'narrative' experience of our lives would make narratives in general easier to comprehend or recall than the content of some expository texts, which may be much less related to life experience. (Norris et al., 2005, p. 554)

This research debate has tended to be in the context of older students and adults where there is an unfortunate lack of suitable science narrative texts upon which to base research enquiries. The arguments have equal weight in the context of young children, for whom there is the advantage of an abundance of texts available for teaching and research.

Finding science-relevant content and contexts as springboards for practical enquiry in the early years is a fairly well-established approach. The wisdom of the choice of building materials used by *The Three Little Pigs* has been subjected to forensic scrutiny. The straw, wood and bricks used by the piglets as building materials can be integrated easily into an exploration of the properties of materials – in this case, their response to the blowing ('huffing and puffing') forces exerted by children (rather than a 'big, bad wolf'). The story has the critical features of narrative described by Norris et al. (2005), the plot concerning the universal theme of using ingenuity to outwit a dark, life-threatening force. The anthropomorphism allows the addition of life-threatening tension to the plot with which children readily identify. Authors use anthropomorphism for different effects. For three little children to be eaten by a wolf might be too gruesome! Yet children often enjoy the tension of dangerous 'cliff hangers' and the comeuppance of sinister villains that can be expressed more acceptably through animal characters.

Reflection

How would you explore children's views of anthropomorphism in children's literature? When, and in what circumstances, are children able to distinguish between fact and fiction in animal characterisations? Do children show awareness that some friendships portrayed would, in nature, be predator–prey relationships? You could think of some examples and talk to children about them.

Some educators may feel that narrative fiction risks introducing 'misconceptions' to children. By contrast, some science education researchers are adopting a different, more analytical approach to children's fiction. Blanquet and

Picholle (2012) explored a story with 4–6 year olds (*Plouf!* by Corentin, 2003). ('Plouf' is onomatopoeic in French, the sound of a pebble dropped into water.) The tale has features in common with Jean de La Fontaine's (2014) *The Wolf And The Fox In The Well*, in which a fox descends a well in a bucket in pursuit of a reflection of the Moon in the water that he has mistaken for cheese. Having discovered his mistake, he lures a wolf into descending in a second bucket from the top at the other end of the rope. The wolf, in pursuit of the same illusory cheese, acts as a counterweight to the fox. The wolf's descent lifts the fox out of the well, leaving the wolf at the bottom as the victim. Corentin's version is more complex, involving a wolf, a pig and a family of rabbits, but the avoidance of being eaten by using a pulley and counterweight remains the central device of the plot. (If English readers wishing to replicate the enquiry find French too great a challenge, de La Fontaine's version is available in translation: www.readbookonline. net/readOnLine/20106/.)

Figure 2.1   Science enquiry stimulated by narrative fiction

Supported by their teachers, children built models to replicate the arrangement in the story. They then compared the predictions of the model within the story with their own empirical observations, commenting on any discrepancies. In fact, Corentin's physics uses artistic licence: it is as fictional as the speech of the animals and cannot be reproduced empirically. As the researchers put it, 'special laws, different from real-world natural laws, govern the fiction'. The children were able to distinguish between the 'two worlds' of fiction and non-fiction and could be readily supported to 'cross the gap between a literary fiction and a real-world experiment' and 'use the results of the latter to confront the predictions of the former' (Blanquet and Picholle, 2012, p. 1908). The researchers suggest that children's capabilities to distinguish between fact and fiction is a key feature of science; their strategy of marrying fiction with science enquiry offers an imaginative way of bringing such distinctions to children's attention.

It makes good sense that the French curriculum explicitly advises the use of children's literature for 'the organisation of interpretative debates' that stimulate imagination and thinking. In another example, Bruguière and Triquet (2014) explored the potential contribution of children's literature to science conceptual understanding by reference to 6–7 year olds' response to *The Tadpole's Promise* (Willis and Ross, 2003). This tale of romance between a tadpole and a caterpillar ends tragically. Although the tadpole promises the caterpillar never to change, once each has metamorphosed into adult form the dénouement sees the frog consume the butterfly. The ostensible tale of romance thinly veils an underlying science narrative of predator–prey relationships, metamorphosis and pond ecology! Once again we see an interaction of fictional and non-fictional frameworks as fertile ground for exploring children's science thinking.

Reflection

What, as science educators, would we want children to take away from the story of *The Tadpole's Promise*, when the love between the caterpillar and tadpole characters grows into a predator-prey relationship? What might children actually derive? Can you envisage how the tale might be used as a jumping-off point for children's further science thinking?

Christopher Wormell's *One Smart Fish* (2011) uses a science framework more deliberately and possibly with a more scientifically didactic intent than the other examples discussed. The tale is of a fish that is clever enough to leave its watery habitat and the company of other fish to venture onto land and learn to walk. Admiration motivates others to follow this lead. The book ends with a double page graphic illustrating myriad creatures evolving in diverse forms to colonise the land, in effect, an image of Darwin's 'Tree of Life'. This story is not a science exposition, but a work of fiction with scientific resonance. In a few pages, the plot draws on roughly 350 million years of the evolutionary history of life on Earth.

Background science

Evolution

Our planet Earth is estimated to be about 4.5 billion years old, with life in the form of the first single-celled organisms emerging roughly 3.8 billion years ago. A landmark event occurred when air-breathing fish moved from shallow water onto land, about 375 million years ago. These vertebrates (animals with backbones) gave rise through very slow evolution over many, many generations to diverse forms: amphibians (needing to return to water to breed); reptiles (including the dinosaurs from which birds later evolved); and mammals, with modern humans in evidence about 0.2 million years ago.

Pause for thought

Science through fiction

Children in the 4-7 year age range engaged with the story of *One Smart Fish*, excitedly suggesting ways that the fish might change as the teacher told the story. Following the story, some 6 and 7 year olds made sequenced drawings to show the fish as it gained the capability to walk on land, followed by further evolutionary changes. Figure 2.2 shows a 6 year old's ideas of how gaining feet was accompanied by changes to the overall body shape, changes to movement from slithering to crawling, and reptiles capable of walking on land.

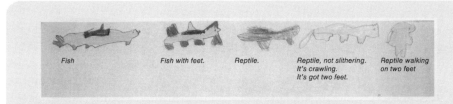

Figure 2.2 A drawn sequence of creatures' evolution from water to land dwelling

Should we, as science educators, feel disquiet that the narrative unfolds with the rules that actually govern the working of the world suspended? Do we need to quickly ensure that children appreciate that, 'Things don't really happen like that! It's just a story!'. As Norris et al. (2005, p. 560) point out, science discourse uses exposition and argumentation to convey reasoning effectively, honestly and with the precision that allows results to be tested through replication by others. Fiction takes liberties, but gets the message across by painting with broad brush strokes.

The justification of narrative fiction as a means of introducing science is irresistible. It can serve to set up a context and stimulate children's interest. Rather like releasing an 'ear worm' into listeners' brains, a work of fiction can initiate a curiosity that might provoke pondering over years to come. Even those uneasy about this use of fiction will need to accept that children will be exposed to these highly successful and popular narratives regardless. As educators, we must come to terms with the fact that explorations in science do not always offer closure. What should we do with a story that takes liberties with the passage of evolutionary time or the physical laws that govern the universe? We take comfort from the reality that it is educators who mediate these stories. Skilled educators 'tell' rather than 'read' stories with inflections of voice, facial expressions and gesture, together with the possible use of props. Adults who know the audience they have captured engage children, pausing to question and confirm understanding. They invite children's predictions, hypotheses and explanations about the words they hear and the images they are shown. Nor need the audience be 'hit cold' with a narrative. Rather, stories can be selected as integral to an educator's wider planning strategy. The possibilities for incisive interventions such as investigations, drawing and modelling activities and supportive interactions during and subsequent to the narrative can be rehearsed. This planning allows the educator to inform her or himself, to identify supporting sources of information: reference books, video, perhaps models or images and background science. Only then do children take possession of the information and transform it so it becomes their own. This is the procedure that gave rise to the child's own image reproduced in Figure 2.2, following a reading of *One Smart Fish*. And of course, there is the motivation that is aroused to explore secondary sources that develop the theme with a more scientific emphasis.

If we find the discrepancy between fact and fiction too troubling, there is the option of avoiding such works altogether, but this would be to overlook the enormous potential of narrative. Jerome Bruner offers some interesting insights into the interface between fact and fiction:

> There are two modes of cognitive functioning, two modes of thought, each providing distinctive ways of ordering experience, of constructing reality. The two (though complementary) are irreducible to one another. Efforts to reduce one mode to the other or to ignore one at the expense of the other inevitably fail to capture the rich diversity of thought. (Bruner, 1986, p. 11)

An example of the 'logico-scientific' mode is a well-constructed logical argument that draws on formal or mathematical systems to explain and describe. An example of the 'narrative' mode is a well-told, convincing story that uses characters who act in various ways to achieve their intentions. The first is universal, the second more about particular connections between events. Either mode can be used as a means of convincing another person of a claim, a truth or an argument. 'Yet what they convince *of* is fundamentally different: arguments convince one of their truth, stories of their lifelikeness' (Bruner, 1986, p. 11).

So here we have it: in teaching science, narrative credibility might serve to orientate children in the direction of factual truths. This strategy is justifiable, but demands a parallel discussion between educators and children as to the distinction between fact and fiction. We feel that it would be a mistake to regard science in the early years curriculum as a discrete, separate and independent subject when the skills developed in the language curriculum clearly have so much to offer to the development of scientific thinking.

The emergence of science-specific capabilities

In the course of the development of a Child Development Assessment Profile designed to be used to record 'whole child' development (3 to 5 years), the authors invited practitioners to collect data pertaining to 1,195 children across about 270 settings. An important feature of the survey was that the data were collected during and as part of practitioners' and children's usual day-to-day interactions. Analysis of this large body of general developmental data enabled the identification of children's emergent science skills within the contexts of wider and more general early years practice (Russell and McGuigan, 2016). The merit of this approach is at least two-fold. Firstly, an overview of general practice can help to identify likely developmental trajectories in science thinking that are so important in a formative pedagogy. Secondly, in identifying educators' existing strengths in their practices, we avoid treating a lack of confidence in teaching science as a professional deficit. We would prefer to build on the positives as growth points. In the early years, all science conceptual understanding is best treated as provisional because that is exactly what it is: interim understanding, temporary and most certainly subject to later elaboration. Understanding will inevitably grow in scope and complexity, so concerns about inadvertently introducing 'misconceptions' lack force (Allen, 2014). All of us who are not professional scientists splash around in our personal oceans of misconceptions but survive and improve our knowledge. Many of the skills deployed by educators and many of the imperfect emerging capabilities shown by children can be thought of as aspects of a progression towards more science-specific understanding. The later science capabilities do not suddenly and spontaneously emerge. By working closely with practitioners, observing, discussing and interpreting practices, we were able to identify antecedent behaviours and, subsequently, routes towards more mature manifestations of the science skills we were interested in nurturing. Working with non-specialist educators and taking into account all aspects of children's development served to support the generation of a number of insights when we reviewed our data using a science education perspective. The qualities of behaviour that could be considered to be precursors of the emergence of science proper we identified in the order 'general developmental', 'science-enabling' and 'science-specific'.

'General developmental' capabilities encompass the familiar 'milestones', including the social, physical and emotional aspects expected of all children. For example, 'attention' tended to be high on the list of practitioners' concerns, particularly for new entrants, and would be a priority from the point of view of a child's socialisation and safety as much as being a necessity for any progress with cognitive skills.

'Science-enabling' behaviours are those judged to have relevance to science because of their generally logico-mathematical nature, but might be equally important to many other subjects and activities. They would tend to support science-relevant activities incidentally rather than with a science focus in mind. Examples would be aspects of numeracy such as measurement (essential to making comparisons in many science activities) and oracy (critical in presenting or interpreting ideas in speech or derived from text).

'Science-specific' behaviours were self-evidently capabilities that the science education literature and science educators describe as such. They would be in evidence when deliberately promoted. However, there were some instances of activities nominally associated with other curricular areas that offered a close correspondence to the requirements of a science curriculum. For example, while all sorting, classifying and measuring activity could be regarded as 'science-enabling', the use of particular set labels such as 'alive', 'was once alive' and 'never alive' tipped the balance into 'science-specific' behaviour. Similarly, some examples of oracy that required clear presentation with reasons of a point of view suggested very close links with the antecedents of argumentation (presenting and defending a point of view with supporting evidence).

Combinations of, and relationships between, these discrete behavioural criteria suggested potential developmental sequences relevant to emergent science. Table 2.1 (adapted from Russell and McGuigan, 2016) includes just some of the criteria and illustrates how some behaviours suggest incremental development (or 'threads' of progress as we named them) as we move down through the right-hand column.

To make sense of and impose order on this complex set of behavioural criteria, we referred to the major guiding principles of science education at the beginning of this chapter, in a form suitable for the early years. This resulted in the summary of behaviours in Figure 2.3: (i) conceptual development (with origins in observation and recording); (ii) enquiry skills (starting from direct experiences); and (iii) science as discourse (beginning with the expression of ideas and moving through 'ideas and evidence' towards argumentation). These are the three areas discussed in greater detail in Chapters 4, 5 and 6. Although discussed individually, the three aspects interact very closely. Opportunities for engaging in them should be recognised as arising in many contexts, including other subjects in the curriculum. They are presented in Figure 2.3 in a manner that confirms their inter-relatedness. In the base tier are the means by which information is acquired once an investigable question has been posed. (Not all children's questions start out as being investigable, but many can be tweaked into a form that can be explored in the real world, rather than only imaginatively.)

Table 2.1 Examples of clustered 'threads' and links with emergent science

Relevance to emergent science	Threads of behaviour and linkages between threads	Example behaviours
General developmental	Paying attention, increasing concentration span and persistence	Listening to and engaging with fictional narrative and imaginary starting points
	Naming and labelling concepts and instances	Naming objects and phenomena accurately
	Expressing ideas	Self-generated ideas expressed with some degree of autonomy and confidence; general language and vocabulary development
Science-enabling	Concrete operational experiences and manipulations; multimodal opportunities	Many of the 'stations' made available in settings (e.g. sand, water, dough, etc.) are designed to ensure basic experiences and particular language and vocabulary development. Opportunities for observation, change and control of materials and events
	Logical operations	Classifying; ordering; comparing similarities and differences; comparing the magnitude of objects and durations of events
	Exploring the nature of materials and making things	Bricollage; experiencing the relationship between the physical and conceptual demands of making
Science-specific	Early explorations and investigations	Children's explorations and more systematic teacher supported enquiries
	Recording outcomes and results	Lists, charts, tables writing, audio, photographs, maps, models, collages, etc.
	Early argumentation	Expressing ideas (a.k.a 'making claims'), drawing conclusions, with justification

Source: Russell, T. and McGuigan, L. (2016). With permission of Springer.

On the left of the base are the secondary sources of evidence that include experts (including teachers), books, films, video or the internet, perhaps even folklore. On the right of the base layer are the (empirical) enquiries that gather data or information using direct techniques such as observation and measurement, including 'fair tests' and other procedures used in enquiries (see Chapter 5). In the central triangle is shown the step in which evidence is appraised for the support it offers, or fails to offer, for the question or problem children have posed (Chapter 6). The question

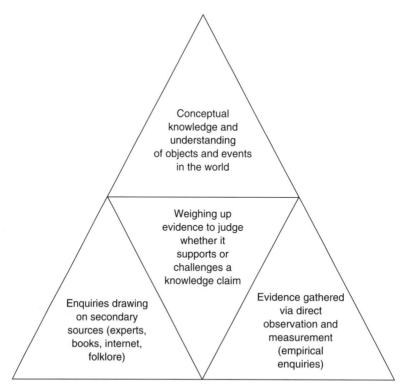

Figure 2.3   How different kinds of knowing in science are inter-related

that is the subject of the enquiry can be considered to imply a claim or proposition for which the enquiry provides evidence that may or may not support it. Conceptual understanding is shown in the apex (see Chapter 4) and will exist both prior to and subsequent to some form of enquiry.

Summary

This chapter has reviewed briefly the background to science for the early years together with some of the important developments in the manner in which it can be addressed.

- The importance of early learning in science for individual achieve-ments and for society in general is a relatively recent innovation dating from around the mid-twentieth century.
- The need for improvement in the science qualifications and training of early years educators is acknowledged by all stakeholders.

- Links between curricular areas should be identified as positive opportunities and explicitly nurtured.
- Narrative story introduces science contexts to early years children in non-threatening, creative, imaginative and meaningful ways, commensurate with children's development.
- Science-specific capabilities can be fostered within the more generalist and holistic practices of early years.
- An increasingly science-specific focus can be planned and implemented as children progress towards the upper age range of the early years phase.

3

Finding out children's ideas

Chapter overview

Here we set out the reasons why exploring the science thinking that children bring with them to their settings and schools prior to any teaching is so important to early years education. Some of the ways teachers might find out children's ideas in the course of daily interactions are suggested and the implications for practice are described. Illustrative examples provide detail as to how the approach might be integrated into everyday practices. Finally, the chapter describes how a constructivist research perspective that examines progression from birth to adulthood informs our understanding of early years practice in science learning.

Why find out children's ideas?

Children actively make sense of their world and form ideas about the people, events and environment around them. Infants and pre-schoolers are already forming their own ideas about how things happen, including some concepts fundamental to scientific thinking. For example, 'object permanence' – the idea that objects continue to exist even when they can no longer be seen – is a fundamental scientific understanding about the constancy of physical objects. Young babies tend to continue to scan visually for objects that have gone out of view, revealing an early appreciation that objects continue to exist when, for example, they move behind a screen. The beginning of understanding of cause and effect, another important awareness with significance to thinking scientifically, is in evidence as children repeatedly release a toy from a high chair and watch it fall to the ground. Over the past two decades there has been an increasing focus on infants' and early years children's understanding of physical objects, living things, materials, the Earth and space as well as attempts to record evidence of early scientific reasoning.

In short, babies and pre-schoolers are forming ideas in their everyday interactions with the world that can be linked to science concepts relevant to biology, physics and chemistry as well as their capabilities to think and act scientifically. Children will bring these ideas to their conversations with early years educators and use them to interpret and pursue new experiences. Finding out and understanding the ideas that children currently hold is an important first step to helping them to make progress (Fleer and Hardy, 2001). Developmentally appropriate practice cannot be simply related to a child's age. It must involve taking into account each child's prior experiences and beliefs as an integral part of planning for their learning.

Some of the accumulated evidence of children's scientific ideas are summarised as learning sequences in Russell and McGuigan (2005), Duschl et al., (2007), Vosniadou (2013) and in the Atlas of Science Literacy (AAAS) project 2061 Volumes I and II (AAAS, 2001, 2007). Sources such as these have mapped out typical developmental learning sequences using the evidence of children's ideas from around three years of age through to the end of formal schooling and beyond. The sequences take account of the very earliest signs of development through to the understanding of the big ideas of science. These sequences are not proposed as hard and fast routes that all learners follow. They are useful in hypothesising fruitful routes forward while avoiding conceptual pitfalls and blind alleys (Russell, 2011, 2015b). Educators' awareness of suggested progressions will sensitise them to certain possibilities and perhaps suggest impediments to understanding that may be unblocked or circumvented. Used in this manner, they are key to a formative approach to pedagogy. Many of the trajectories described do not claim to be the last word on matters and many sequences may be tentative. They will be revised as information collected by educators from children's different experiences is combined with insights into effective teaching strategies.

There are several key reasons for adults to take children's ideas seriously:

- All children must become accustomed to the fact that, when given time and space to stop and think, they have ideas that they can express. Some may too easily become habituated to saying, 'I don't know', as the result of uncertainty or a lack of adult expectation. Adults need to believe that children have ideas and that, with encouragement, they can express them. Conversations with children in a relaxed context will readily confirm this assumption.
- Children's ideas (and often adults' views also) are very often different from conventional science explanations. Having an idea of some kind and making it explicit is preferable to responses such as, 'I have no idea!'. A starting idea overcomes the inertia of incomprehension. Once expressed, it is something to work with.
- Children's ideas tend to be firmly held and difficult to change because they work for them and make sense to them. They may not change as a result of an adult's head-on attempt to impose a different, more orthodox, understanding. A challenge from a position of adult authority may come across as disempowering. One person's 'proof' will not have any impact on another whose starting assumptions are quite different. More subtle strategies are needed.
- Children's developing ideas can be seen by educators as sequences or learning pathways that help to describe the course of learning. A formative and developmental pedagogy requires assessment – finding out what children think currently – as an important first step to knowing how to advance that understanding. The starting point for any intervention must always be children's current understanding. Only then does differentiated treatment according to need become a possibility.

Research informed by 'constructivist' theory (a cognitive perspective on how knowledge and understanding are constructed) has contributed insights into how to elicit and make sense of children's ideas about science. The research has also informed our understanding of conceptual progression in science (what the ideas are and the typical sequences via which they develop); the ordering of teaching and learning interventions; the logical relations between ideas that inform curriculum development; and, not least, provided guidelines for assessment by suggesting what is realistic to expect children to understand at different times in their progress. There have also been initiatives to promote relevant pedagogies through curriculum materials that build on this approach, for example, Nuffield Primary Science (Black et al., 1993, 1995). Though curriculum content changes and varies between countries and over time, the pedagogical approach remains valid in all contexts.

Pause for thought

Constructivism

The term 'constructivism' is used by psychologists to describe the theoretical approach to studying how children construct knowledge from direct experiences. This can occur independently of adult support or intervention. Some researchers prefer to refer to 'social constructivism', their interest and emphasis being on how social groups and society at large induct individuals into shared understanding as a communal process. Sharing ready-made meanings through language is a good example. Others use the term 'constructionist', mostly in the context of IT and associated with the writing of Seymour Papert (1994). Constructionists emphasise building things publicly, in the world, perhaps digitally, as contrasted with constructing personal internal mental models. All these approaches are 'constructivist'.

Inhelder and Piaget (1958) researched 'natural' or informal, self-regulated encounters with the physical world, avoiding learning mediated by social interventions and formal instruction. In the same tradition, constructivist thinkers describe the young learner as actively forming ideas through personal sense-making while engaged in direct experiences of the world. Development in thinking can happen when a new experience challenges or conflicts with existing ideas. When the learner encounters a discrepancy in the form of the incompatibility of two ideas, an internal cognitive struggle is brought about to make sense of the new experience and regain mental equilibrium. This struggle in the course of conceptual change is referred to as 'cognitive conflict'. Many, but not all, of the approaches to helping children change their ideas can be linked to the idea that revision in children's understanding can be brought about by a challenge in which new information conflicts with existing ideas (see Chapter 1).

Other educational researchers have emphasised the social influences on children's ideas: interactions with teachers, parents, peers and wider culture. The social context of learning is the major focus in such perspectives. The phrase 'Zone of Proximal Development' or ZPD was developed by Vygotsky (1962) to elucidate what a child can understand and achieve alone and what might be possible with adult and peer support. Current understandings are referred to as actual development whereas the level children might attain next, with support, is referred to as the ZPD. Eliciting children's thinking reveals actual development, what is understood, what has been achieved and what children can accomplish without help. Finding out ideas also helps to reveal what children are beginning to understand and what understanding they are likely to be capable of grasping, given appropriate support. That support may be through interactions with peers or tailored adult intervention. This way of formulating the process of learning helps to shape the kind of encounters that educators can design as challenges, which is why finding out ideas is such a crucial first step in planning children's learning. The strategy of designing focused learning activities on the basis of current understandings is referred to as 'formative assessment pedagogy'. The approach includes cycles of finding out ideas and the provision of appropriate interventions. These challenges must meet children's needs in the sense of causing them to think and make progress in their understanding and skills while avoiding overwhelming them. A more detailed discussion of the formative assessment cycle is presented in Chapter 8.

The rationale for finding out ideas has presented the key elements of constructivist thinking to show why we favour a formative approach. Armed with this theoretical understanding, practitioners can choose to embed the techniques as an integral part of their practice. Once strategies for finding out children's ideas are incorporated into everyday holistic practices, constructivism can become spontaneous, wide-ranging and responsive to unexpected situations as they arise. The interactive, interpersonal freedom of the approach brings teaching to life.

Helping children to feel safe and confident to express ideas

An overarching aim in every setting and classroom is to establish a safe learning environment. When this has been established, the expression and exchange of ideas can happen anywhere and everywhere, affecting all interactions. The techniques then become a pervading influence on the ethos of the environment rather than 'bolted on' attempts to find out ideas. It is acknowledged that young children can be shy and reticent and early years practitioners encourage them to find their voice as soon as possible. To this end, it is useful to believe that ideas can be expressed in a variety of ways in a range of situations: talking, drawing, modelling and constructions, movement, drama and role-play (see Chapter 4). Developing such a culture requires agreement between adults on the approaches to be adopted to foster young, confident learners. Children feel at ease speaking to adults once a relaxed, friendly and conversational style has been established, with confirmation of adults' keen interest in all points of view. The time this takes will depend on the personality and experience of each child and the skills of the adults with whom they will learn to interact.

For many children, separation from parents and carers is unproblematic. In contrast, on initial entry, some children may be in awe and apprehensive of adults, older children, unfamiliar surroundings and the absence of their customary carer. The strangeness of the environment may be inhibiting and drain confidence, however warm and well-meaning the staff. When children have delayed or restricted language development, this situation may be exacerbated, so that drawing children out to discuss their needs and preferences becomes more complicated. Experienced staff will have learned to be vigilant but outwardly calm, ensuring that any distress shown by children does not escalate. The routine of the wider group will be maintained while encouraging the newcomers' participation through encouraging actions and conversations. The approaches described in the following paragraphs develop further this theme of helping children to feel comfortable in transactions with others centred on their own ideas and finding their own voice.

How do you find out children's ideas?

Elicitation or 'finding out ideas' techniques can take a variety of forms, limited only by our imagination and creativity as educators and communicators. Incidentally, while our focus is on the development of early scientific thinking, other aspects of children's developmental journeys are also intimately bound up in the interactions described. The revelation of what is going on inside children's mind-brains marks the beginning of an exciting learning journey for the educator and the child.

Non-directive questioning and open-ended discussions

One of the enduring legacies of the way early constructivist researchers such as Piaget (1973) investigated children's thinking was the application of a technique called the 'clinical interview', so called because of its diagnostic intention. Non-directive techniques imply that any question posed avoids inadvertently offering clues to an expected answer. The adult presents situations and poses 'open' questions. These convey a genuine interest in children's ideas and avoid suggesting a response or any tendency to lead children step-by-step (either by word or gesture) towards a particular response. The task presented must be sufficiently structured to maintain the focus of interest and generate unambiguous outcomes. Responses to children's ideas must be acknowledged with empathy and interest. A conversational style is used that includes follow-up questions to pursue a train of thought.

Consider the following example of a task to check understanding of number conservation: two sets of sweets of equal number are presented in two rows, with a clear one-to-one correspondence in their alignment. Children's appreciation of the equivalence of the two sets is confirmed by asking whether the number of sweets in each row is the same. One row of sweets is then stretched out beyond the initial configuration and the questions asked as to whether the number of sweets in the elongated row is now, 'more, less, or the same?' as originally presented. This exemplifies how the child's understanding of number conservation is pursued quite closely in a structured manner, without leading the response. (Non-conservers of number will suggest that the elongated row with the same sweets now contains more sweets than the shorter row. Number conservation is typically in evidence at around 6–7 years of age.)

Another form of non-directive technique derives from psychotherapeutic interview where the therapist wishes to elicit the patient's state of mind without 'putting ideas in her head'. Very simply, ideas are reflected back, repeated more or less verbatim.

Patient: 'I'm really sad and upset'.

Therapist: 'You're feeling sad and upset?'

The reflection back to the subject of her own sentiment using a questioning tone invites further comment, an elaboration, although tacitly so. In a similar manner, when a child suggests that a leaf has 'gone rusty', the questioning response, 'You think the leaf has gone rusty?' is likely to elicit expansion. If not, a further prompt might take the form, 'What makes you think the leaf has gone rusty?'. Quite possibly, an association with water or with the change in colour might emerge. By contrast, for the adult to follow her own line of reasoning by introducing an association of rust with (ferrous) metal would be ill advised, because it would influence (we would say 'contaminate') the child's thinking. 'Do you think there is metal in the leaf?' would be a leading question because it introduces an idea outside the child's thinking. Coming from an adult who is taking an interest, the idea of the presence of metal in the leaf could be disproportionately influential. This would be unfortunate as the child might have been using 'rusty' simply in the sense of 'the colour of rust'.

Early years teachers can adopt this non-directive questioning style to elicit ideas without putting ideas in children's heads. Used judiciously, the procedure can help even the most reticent children to find their voice.

Reflection

Try having conversations with a child (or a colleague or friend) in which you listen with interest to their expressed ideas and refrain from adding any additional information. Do this by encouraging them to tell you more by reflecting back to them in a questioning manner what they tell you. What effect do you feel this has on the way the conversation proceeds? How easy or difficult do you find it to refrain from adding your own ideas? How does the experience compare with normal conversations you have with people?

Strategies that are deliberately open-ended in the sense that they encourage children to contribute and offer alternative ideas might include the following opening question stems:

- What do you think we could use … [to make a shelter for the snail?]
- How do you think we could … [get the water to go a long way through the pipes?]
- What do you think we might find … [when we take a walk in the woods?]
- Which animals do you think we might see … [at the farm?]
- Why do you think … [some seeds haven't started to grow?]

The educator is setting an agenda, arousing interest and empowering children by using questions that assume they have something to say that is valuable and worth listening to. Being asked our point of view is implicitly an indication of esteem.

Initially, children may be reluctant to reveal their thinking. The message for practitioners is to refuse to accept evasions such as, 'I don't know', but to gently encourage children to make the effort to search their experience, delve into their imagination. To generate a response takes far more effort than to fend off requests for an idea – at least, it does until the habit of mind is established of reflective imagination. Waiting patiently for the child's response is a productive strategy. The 'wait time' allowed for children to answer a teacher's question is often barely a few seconds (Black and Wiliam, 1998a, 1998b) and extending it is a way of increasing the likelihood of input from the more reticent voices. Teachers we have worked with in getting to grips with this approach often comment that one important aspect they learned was the need to spend more time listening to children and rather less time talking.

Discussions in the context of real materials

Real materials and direct experiences are always available wherever there is early years provision. As children handle concrete objects and materials, engaging and meaningful starting points for discussion arise almost inevitably. A concrete referent that all parties to the discussion can see and handle avoids any ambiguity about the subject of conversation and can provide a scaffold for the discussion. Children can point to the features they wish to refer to when descriptive vocabulary fails them. The direct experiences that might be drawn upon may be planned events, while at other times unplanned, naturally occurring events that excite children's curiosity. The common feature is the intent to use the physical experience to spark a conversation that draws children out and encourages self-expression. Conversations may be one-to-one or involve a group of children, the more reticent ones gradually being drawn in while avoiding undue attention or any sense of pursuit by the adult.

Pause for thought

Exploring real materials

Evie and Jack aged 3 years are in the nursery, exploring soft modelling clay and simple tools such as shaped cutters that have captured their

Figure 3.1   Exploring soft modelling clay

attention. The activity is likely to be familiar and as such, comforting, particularly to children new to the group. Ways of exploring and handling clay are intuitively accessible to children and might stimulate modelling of objects, events or scenarios that children and adults could discuss in a conversational style.

Educators may observe children and pose carefully framed questions. 'How does the clay feel? What shapes can you make? What happens when you squeeze it?' The adult must take care not to assail children with questions, focusing on the children's actions to encourage comments and helping them to feel at ease. Relevant to their understanding of forces and materials is the possibility of children demonstrating in their actions and speech some of the ways in which clay might be shaped, twisted, stretched and cut. In the course of their discussions, the adult may gently check whether they have the vocabulary to label their shapes. Opportunities will also arise to explore their ideas about what they have made and how they achieved certain effects. Although ostensibly the activity is about manipulation and making physical products, there is a significant dimension in the form of interpersonal communications and the generation of ideas. The relaxed ambience facilitates unguarded exchanges with children who might feel threatened and confronted in less informal situations. In this climate, it may be possible for the adult to use careful questioning to take the discussion in productive directions.

Pause for thought

Outdoors kitchen

Direct experiences can be arranged to encourage children to talk together and to exchange views. The 'outdoors kitchen area' encourages a variety of discussions and interactions as the girl and boy in Figure 3.2, aged 3 and 4 years respectively, mix and 'bake' different 'ingredients' of their choosing.

The resources, including pans, baking cases, trays, saucepans, etc., are not toys but are real utensils donated by parents. Boxes and crates serve as shelving, cooker and seats. The area is deliberately restricted, just as in a real kitchen, to encourage negotiation as children move about

(Continued)

(Continued)

Figure 3.2   Experiencing some of the ways materials can be changed in the outdoors or 'mud' kitchen

the space. The resources are left outdoors at the end of each day. Children use the naturally found materials at hand for their ingredients: soil, sand, twigs, leaves and water. They exchange ideas about their intentions for the different materials and how they might be changed by mixing: whether the mud is runny or thick and stiff. Their vocabulary reveals awareness of some of the ways materials can be changed, including 'cooking' 'freezing', 'boiling', 'baking'. Ideas about healthy and unhealthy diets might emerge as children describe some of the foods and meals being prepared. There is scope for children to propose ideas about quantities, measurement and number as they begin to pay attention to the amounts of their ingredients in spoons and cups, or count the number of spoonfuls of water, or estimate the time needed to bake their muffins. Later, additional resources might be provided to boost the chances of standard measurement: balance scales, tape measures, jugs and timers. While children's ownership of the activity is important in giving their imaginations full rein, it is anticipated that adults will, from time to time, engage children to discuss their emerging ideas and help to influence the direction of children's focus.

Background science

Origins of materials

One of the first distinctions to be made in thinking about materials is between the object and the substance from which that object is made. Materials can be classified in a range of ways, including reference to the name by which they are known (wood, paper, metal, etc.); the material's properties (shiny, transparent, hard, sharp, etc.); or according to origins (natural and manufactured) or uses, behaviour or function (floats, magnetic, waterproof, see through, etc.).

Making the most of unusual or spontaneous events

Unexpected spontaneous events may be as rich or even richer than those that have been pre-planned. Educators may take advantage of occurrences such as naturally occurring unusual weather conditions to find out children's ideas.

Pause for thought

Ideas about ice

An overnight sharp fall in temperature outside the nursery resulted in ice being formed on water troughs in the outdoor area.

(Continued)

(Continued)

Figure 3.3 Learning by observing and exploring

The frozen surfaces caught the teacher's attention and, curious as to what sense children might make of this event, she encouraged her 3 year olds to handle and investigate the ice, anticipating tremendous opportunities for exploring vocabulary. Some children described the ice initially as both 'soft' and 'hard', suggesting a commonly held confusion amongst young children between 'soft' and 'smooth' (but hard). Their ideas were followed up later by collecting objects and putting them into sets of 'soft', 'hard', 'rough', 'smooth' and discussing the overlapping of some of these attributes.

When one child dropped a large piece of ice, the children seemed to take the fact that it shattered in their stride, gathering up the splinters.

One of the children wanted to take his fragments of ice home and suggested he would 'put them in mummy's bag' to keep the ice from melting. This proposition led to the involvement of the entire group, prompted by their teacher, in putting forward ideas about how the pieces could be kept from melting as long as possible. Recognising the opportunities for further exploration, the teacher encouraged discussion of the different ideas children had about the properties of ice. She helped them to shape their ideas about melting ice into enquiries. Together, they agreed to leave pieces of ice in bowls in the freezer, in the fridge and on the cupboard. Some thought wrapping ice like ice lollies might stop it melting, so some ice was wrapped in paper before placing it on the windowsill. Children were encouraged to look at the ice during the session and to talk about any changes they observed. Encouraging children to handle the ice drew their attention to the changes and helped them to compare the ice and water. Some children drew pictures of the water forming in the bowl.

Background science

Three states of matter

Materials occur in three states: solid, liquid or gas, depending on their temperature (or energy level). Only a very few substances are familiar to us in all three states – that is, within the range of temperatures at which people can survive. Water is one such substance, being familiar as ice (solid), water (liquid) and as a gas (water vapour). Steam comprises tiny droplets of water whereas water vapour is invisible. The change from one state to another is 'reversible', meaning that it is a physical change in which the essential nature of the substance – the particles of which it is comprised – remains the same. In irreversible changes, the nature of the substance itself is changed, for example by different kinds of particles combining when heated.

Drawings of ideas

We have so far described approaches that encourage the expression of ideas through discussion, but there are other ways of accessing children's thinking. Two-dimensional representations – photographs, paintings, drawings, signs, diagrams and so forth – are extremely prevalent in human society and often a more accessible mode of expression than words or text. The message transmitted by an image can be understood instantaneously, which is why they are used to signal information needing an immediate response, such as danger. Diagrams can be more complex, requiring more effort in their decoding.

We find it useful to define several different qualities of drawing produced by children. The distinction between them will be apparent to educators rather than to the children who generate them, at least initially. 'Observational drawings' are attempts to capture a likeness in the form of a pictorial representation of the important features of the object depicted, something approaching an exact copy. This may require the image to be simplified as compared with a photographic reproduction, so that the salient features stand out clearly. In 'imaginative drawing' the constraints of reproducing what appears before the eyes are relaxed and fantasy can play a role. A third possibility, and an extremely important and useful one in the context of children's science understanding, is the possibility of depicting ideas about things, rather than reproductions or fantasies. Drawings and diagrams can be used very effectively to convey ideas about objects and events that might not be visible. The important feature may be intangible or invisible (such as sound, smell or energy). Children nonetheless have ideas about abstract and difficult to access contexts. These ideas might be about how plants grow, what is happening inside an incubating egg, how the hidden mechanism of a clockwork toy causes it to move, how sound travels, how the washing on a line dries, the positions of the Earth and the Sun that give rise to night and day, and so on.

Drawings of these events are capable of conveying a whole spectrum of relationships of different kinds: relative size of component parts; time; causal relations and relative directions of movement; and other abstract or invisible traits. Sequenced drawings or picture strip sketches (Chapter 4) enable children to demonstrate their ideas about events that take place over time such as, 'What will happen to the ice during a day?' or 'How might a fossil have been formed?'. Children will respond to the invitation of producing drawings of such scenarios with little hesitation, perhaps being even more receptive to the challenge than adults. Drawings provide an overt, concrete basis for discussions between children and between children and adults. It may come as a surprise that young children can communicate an abstract science idea through the medium of drawing, but there should be no doubt. We have confirmed this capability innumerable times. The spoken elaboration may add detail to what is conveyed. It may be essential to the adult's interpretation. Where they are able, children may add their written explanations, or if they cannot express themselves in writing, an adult might annotate the image with children's dictated thoughts or explanations.

Pause for thought

Drawing ideas about making sounds

In this example, children had made sound makers and Mia (aged 7) was asked to draw a picture to show her ideas of how she could hear the sound coming from the other side of a closed door. The edge of the door is drawn as the vertical rectangle in her drawing, with a child shown the other side of the door moving the shaker (Figure 3.4). She explained her drawing: 'It's going through the cracks above the door and under the door there's a space ... and it goes round and round in here'.

The pathway of the sound is shown in dotted lines leaving the 'shaker' and travelling through the gaps around the door to the adjacent room. On arrival, the musical notation of quavers is used to suggest

Figure 3.4 A drawing of ideas about how sound travels

(Continued)

(Continued)

that the sound is audible. The drawn representation, elaborated through discussion, reveals this child's notion (and it is a familiar one, see Watt and Russell, 1990) that sound moves through space, provided it is unimpeded. The scientific explanation for sound travelling is very different and in fact, counter-intuitive. Sound needs a medium through which to travel – usually air, but solids or liquids also transmit sound.

Within the early years curricula there is much potential for exploring sound through making music. Children making and explaining their own music makers might provide jumping-off points for an investigation of the (scientifically incorrect) idea that sound needs gaps to pass through in order to be heard.

Background science

Sound

Sound is made when objects move or vibrate. Hitting an object such as a drum harder increases the volume of sound because the drum skin vibrates more. Sound waves travel though air like the ripples when a stone is dropped into a pond, but in 3-D. The waves are compressions and rarefactions that can travel through solids, liquids or gases, but not through a vacuum. Sound does not follow a single path from the source of the sound to the ear: it spreads out in all directions. As it moves away from the source, it spreads out over a wider and wider area and becomes fainter as sound energy is dissipated.

3-D models to reveal ideas

Children are likely to have built up ideas about animals through direct experiences, through zoo visits and looking after pets as well as secondary sources, including stories and TV. Early explorations are likely to focus on observing animals, considering their appearance, needs and behaviours and thinking about how they might be cared for and protected. Developing an understanding of and respect for animals is an important part of the early years curriculum. Making 3-D models offers children new perspectives for making public their understanding in a manner that may not be available to them in other modes. A model allows the whole of the animal in the round to be available for discussion. The essential attributes to be included and the relative position and size of different features can be made explicit. In the example below, the child calls upon (and reveals) assumptions about the conditions that snails need in order to live as she constructs a 'home' for a snail.

Pause for thought

Using 3-D models

Hettie (aged 3) has built a 'house' for a snail she has found in the outdoor area.

Figure 3.5 Creating a habitat for a snail

(Continued)

(Continued)

   She has collected together the materials she wants to use and describes her reasoning to her teacher. 'Plant pots to keep the rain and wind out; grass for food and a bottle top carefully filled with water because the snail will be thirsty and like a drink'. The holes in the top of the pot allow Hettie to look inside to check to 'see the snail is happy'. Hettie reveals awareness that the snail will need food and water to live. Her use of anthropomorphic language shows how she draws on her knowledge of the needs of people as inferences about the snail's needs.

Children's tendency to describe animals in terms of human characteristics was reported by Carey (1985) and Inagaki and Hatano (2002). While children were found to use anthropomorphic reasoning to describe the animals they were observing, according to Thulin and Pramling (2009), it was adults who wanted to engage children's attention who often introduced it.

Using writing to find out ideas

Older children within the early years age group might be encouraged to express their ideas in writing. Writing provides the teacher and children with a permanent trace of their thinking that can be returned to for discussion. There is the possibility of considering the reasons for points of view being different from an earlier record. This may convince children that their ideas are changing and that they are making progress.

   Children's written ideas might be put together to form a group record, possibly by making floor books – large collections of their ideas in writing and drawing. 'Idea Walls' offer another way to present a volume of children's work for subsequent reference. Both of these modes can be an immense source of pride to their authors, deliberately constructed to a large scale so that children can view one another's contributions and add comments. Such collections can be extended throughout a topic, building a comprehensive formative and summative record of children's achievements (see Chapter 8). Christine Howe's research (Howe, 2014) confirms that differences between children's ideas are a significant facilitating factor in their learning. Encouraging children to return to their earlier products and discuss what different people contributed offers far more than mere opportunities for nostalgia and pride. Howe has proved that group learning continues for some considerable time after the 'live' event, as ideas 'sink in' or as discrepancies within or between children are reconciled. This insight from Howe's research is of enormous importance for early years practice.

Responding to children's ideas

The manner in which adults respond to children's often partially-formed utterances is important. It should be assumed that children are as sensitive and aware as adults to both verbal and non-verbal reactions. Adults should give a warm acceptance to the children's ideas, perhaps in the form of a comment such as, 'that's interesting', or 'lovely thinking', or non-verbally with a smile or thumbs up. Such responses communicate respect for children's viewpoints without suggesting that they are either correct or incorrect. These positive signals enhance children's sense of self-worth and positive views of themselves as learners. Expressions of unconditional positive regard establish trust and are a form of professional response to children's ideas that can be readily applied in practice. Concept cartoons (Naylor and Keogh, 2013) and puppets (Simon et al., 2008) might also be used to help model and encourage children's positive verbal and non-verbal responses to expressed ideas.

Key features of approaches to finding out ideas

All the approaches to finding out ideas include the following key features.

- Children must be made to feel safe and self-confident enough to express their thoughts. In an early years context it is equally important that other children be guided to show consideration and empathy in listening to, and making the effort to understand, others' points of view.
- Children have to establish the conviction that they really do have ideas of their own. Some children might enter settings and classrooms from an environment in which there is no precedent for any such appreciation.
- Children have to learn that other children also have minds, thoughts and ideas and that those ideas may differ from their own.
- Adults have to believe that children's ideas are an essential ingredient of a responsive pedagogy, an aspect that adds value to the experiences offered, not simply odd or amusing contributions to be acknowledged before the real business of teaching begins.

- Adults must appreciate that listening is at least as important as speaking. Children need to be actively attended to by adults and other children. All thoughtful contributions need to be respected. Adults will need to model attentive listening.
- Adults and children create a much richer educational environment once they acknowledge and exploit the fact that different modes of communication offer different expressive affordances. Different ways of expressing ideas reveal different insights and understandings.

Summary

This chapter emphasised the importance of finding out children's ideas as being at the heart of pedagogy. The practices that may be employed by early years educators to elicit and support children's expression of their thoughts were reviewed.

- Children bring a tremendous variety of ideas about the world to their early years environments. Educators should assume that prior understandings have a strong bearing on further learning.
- While spoken and written language are important and often pre-eminent, other modes of expression may reveal the full spectrum of understanding.
- Learning is understood to involve qualitative changes in thinking as children develop and extend their experiences, and likewise, the modes of making those ideas explicit.
- The formative approach to learning we describe is one that highlights the importance of finding out children's ideas as integral to the nurturing of emergent science thinking.

4

Developing conceptual understanding in science

Chapter overview

This chapter describes how early years settings endeavour to extend children's experiences through use of all their senses. In particular, means of nurturing conceptual development by extending the modalities that children might be encouraged to use in making sense of their encounters with the physical world are discussed.

The role of direct experiences in conceptual development

Both indoors and outdoors, early provision regularly offers youngsters opportunities to engage with materials: water, sand, clay, foam, slime and 'mini-worlds' of models as well as all manner of 2-D and 3-D construction materials. Real-world objects are also collected, examined and displayed, with observations recorded. These perceptions of thought-provoking objects, materials and events give rise to the need for vocabulary development. For example, different qualities of sand need to be described. They might be 'gritty', 'lumpy', 'grey', 'damp', 'dry', 'fine', 'coarse' or 'runny'. These attributes may affect how sand behaves when handled and so, incidentally, thinking about handling properties introduces the ways that materials are classified. If only encountered passively, these direct sensations derived from experiences may not serve as learning events. It is during interactions around the experiences, with other children and with adults, that children will be helped to make meanings. By engaging with and reflecting upon such experiences, children develop various categorisation systems. In many cases, these will be similar to the classifications that scientists also use: size, colour, texture, temperature, mass, sound, use, and so on. Classifying and naming is important in agreeing the characteristics of things, allowing ideas to be shared reliably between people. Subtle distinctions despite similarities in appearance can be important and become even more so through life, as in the distinctions between gold and fool's gold, diamond and lead crystal, or between edible and poisonous mushrooms. Children can learn and communicate the knowledge that, to be moulded and made into sandcastles, sand needs to be not too dry, nor too wet, but just damp enough. Agreeing named attributes of things allows ideas or 'concepts', as we are calling them, to be shared. In playing with sand, tactile observation plays a key role in learning about the material, predicting its behaviour and using the knowledge acquired purposefully. Note that the term 'observation' as used in the context of science education refers to all the senses that can be used to gather information. Handling sand can involve sight, touch, maybe hearing and possibly smell.

The experience of engagement in science activities will feel seamless to children. In contrast, the analysis of the different components of scientific behaviour and which is to the fore in any given activity presents an array of possibilities to educators. Deconstructing activities allows us to consider the mental and physical processes involved in each element of learning science, and consequently, how each may be developed. Seeing science opportunities as potentially present at any time makes such scrutiny even more useful. In this chapter, the focus is on how the ideas of science are learned. These science ideas are the 'stuff' of science, the *conceptual* understanding or 'subject matter content knowledge'. Acquisition of conceptual understanding requires a focus on the 'what' of science, the particular ideas that constitute biology, chemistry and physics knowledge, such as ideas about particular animals and plants, materials and phenomena.

To examine what is involved in conceptual development, we can begin with a definition of a concept as 'an idea formed in the mind-brain'; a mapping between what is outside and what develops inside the head. The process of internalising necessitates some form of transformation, some way of re-representing the world's physical objects and processes as the mental phenomena we know as ideas. A science concept will have been arrived at through experiences that allow a learner to order and classify an instance and to make a generalisation. An example relevant to children's developing understanding in the early years is the concept of 'living things' or what it is to be 'alive'. There is evidence that by 3 years children form views that help them to distinguish between some living things and artefacts (Gelman, 2003; Greif et al., 2006). Greif et al. (2006) found that the questions children (3–5 years) ask reveal insights into what they count as important characteristics of living and inanimate objects. They were found to be much more likely to ask questions of the kind that probed *uses* of the artefacts. In contrast, they posed questions about food choices, location and reproduction, etc. to find out more about unfamiliar animals. The questions children posed suggest an awareness of relevant biological characteristics that may contribute to a developing understanding of living things.

Background science

Characteristics of living things

To be considered living things, organisms must meet the seven criteria of movement, reproduction, sensitivity, growth, respiration, excretion, and nutrition.

A way of encouraging children to think about being 'alive' is to arrange for them to engage in classifying things, preferably real objects, so that each individual in a discussion is aware of exactly what is being discussed. We might all agree that a parrot squawking in its cage is alive, whereas referring to a photograph or a stuffed soft toy requires clarification of the ambiguity: the image is not alive but the animal represented might be. To avoid this uncertainty, an adult could point to real objects around the room, naming the objects, and posing the question, 'Is X alive?', or even better, draw attention to objects encountered outdoors and asking, 'Is that [tree, bird, leaf, stone, Sun, wind, grass, stick, stream, pond, wooden gate] alive? How do we know?'. The targets of the questioning should include clear set and non-set members as well as introducing uncertainties that serve to sharpen criteria for set inclusion or exclusion. Referring to real objects outdoors, from oak trees to ants, ensures that the size of items and their mobility is not a limiting factor. The sky is, literally, the limit.

Pause for thought

The meaning of 'alive'

Digging in the soil, the 3 year old child in Figure 4.1 found a small stick and showed it to the adult nearby.

Figure 4.1   Is it alive?

Instances in which children muster the confidence to approach carers with an object or material they have found are relatively common in the early years. The teacher welcomed the child's initiative and identified it as an opportunity to explore his ideas about the found object. She adjusted her position to the child's level to signal her interest and to coax a conversation in which they could begin to examine the features of and identify the object he had found. Holding the item in her outstretched hand, she gestured with the other hand to invite him to feel the object. The teacher showed in the way that she reached out to the child and in her questioning that she was interested in the ideas he may have about the object. The child was clearly at ease. He smiled and pressed the object in response before quietly offering a few words, 'Is it a worm?'. (Other children had dug up worms and he clearly would have liked to have had similar success, to the extent that his observation might have been distorted.) The child's suggestion led to further discussion of living and non-living things. Later, children's collections of sticks, stones, leaves, seeds, etc. found in the soil were discussed and sorted into groups of 'living' and 'not living' objects.

Reflection

Select a science concept that you intend to introduce to young children. Explore your own understanding of the idea by thinking it through to the limits of your personal comprehension. Map out your ideas briefly to identify what you think are the most important facets of the concept. Draw linking lines between these facets with a few words added to explain the nature of each link. (Your drawing is actually known as a 'concept map'. You can add to it as you develop your understanding.) Where you are able, include evidence for your understanding in the form of brief descriptions of *how* you know *what* you know. Pinpoint your uncertainties and consider how you might resolve these.

Giving explicit reasons for set membership is an essential component of any science concept classification activity, so justification should be integral to this form of discourse. But children may feel their conceptual understanding is so self-evident as not to require any reason or back up. (Or maybe they just want to get on with something else that they find more interesting!) A reason needs to be requested or cajoled when it is not forthcoming. A stone, for example, may evoke the justification, 'Everyone knows a stone isn't alive!' or 'I just know!'. These refusals to provide explanations are not acts of reasoning and we should resist acquiescing to this evasiveness. Though the everyday way of communicating tends to be much looser, science tries to be more exact (accurate rather than pedantic) in establishing definitions. Justifications for the 'self-evident' set members of any concept should be pursued so as to elicit the criteria the child has in mind. The value of this strategy emerges when set inclusion decisions become more difficult, at which time criteria elicited previously can be used as a checklist for decision making. A number of recurring ideas, well-documented in the research literature, will certainly emerge. Some surprising items are likely to be deemed to be alive, including fire, rivers, streams and clouds (Carey, 1985).

The 'funny ideas' that children reveal have been called 'preconceptions', 'misconceptions', 'alternative conceptions' and have proved so fascinating that they have spawned voluminous research activity over several decades, most intensively during the 1980s and 1990s. A significant bibliography of over 8,000 entries of reported research was compiled at the Leibniz Institute for Science and Mathematics Education at the University of Kiel (IPN) (Duit, 2009). Along with a number of other researchers who have worked in this area, 'misconception' would not be our favoured choice of description. In the primary phase especially, but throughout 'school science', science understanding is likely to be provisional and imperfect, an approximation to scientifically accurate explanations. In other words, there are likely to be as many misconceptions as there are children's ideas (AAAS, 2001, 2007; Duit, 2009; Allen, 2014).

The criteria for classification decisions are more likely to be expressed once the habit of children stating justifications has been established. This will only happen if there is an adult expectation that they should do so. For instance, the idea of movement in many natural objects may cause children to suppose those items, such as fire, are alive. Fire sucks in air, propagates itself, needs fuel to burn and moves by itself. These are persuasive reasons to believe a flame is a living thing. Children's ruminating on their own explicit criteria is the only certain way for them to reorganise their ideas. Adults can support this process using dialogic strategies that encourage reflection by asking for reasons for expressed beliefs. Imposed adult corrections, such as, 'No! Fire is not alive!', are just illusory solutions if nothing changes inside children's heads. Furthermore, such interjections may erode children's willingness to express themselves in future, for fear of being 'wrong'. Classification of 'alive' poses more challenges when the focus is on objects that were once alive but are no longer so: wooden furniture, cotton clothing, cork, rubber, bone and teeth (prior to being left for the Tooth Fairy, perhaps) are all useful examples to discuss. The conceptual demand increases because knowledge of the object prior to its current appearance has to be taken into account. This wider information is not directly observable. It has to be gained through life experiences or secondary sources of information. Such sources include knowledgeable adults, books and websites that children may not yet have encountered.

Pause for thought

Refining concepts

Harriet is about 21 months and is vocalising with sounds that approximate spoken words. These utterances are clearly recognisable to those who know her well. She has a set of brightly coloured stubby wax crayons that she uses frequently, often while sitting with a parent, drawing and colouring. Adults are very impressed that she is able to select the correct crayon when asked, 'Please will you give me the green?', or any of the other colours. It is tempting to believe that she has a concept of 'green', 'red', 'yellow', etc. Her successes are applauded and she beams with pleasure in response. On another occasion during the same time of her life, she was scrunching and kicking her way through brightly coloured autumn leaves, enjoying the sounds, shapes, colours and the actions. When asked to pick up a red leaf and separately, a yellow leaf, her response was not automatic, as with the crayons. She looked around, seemingly puzzled by the request. An explanation might be that she had not yet developed the concept of 'red' in a general sense. Without doubt, she could pick out 'red crayon', but it seems likely that her representation at that time was of what we might call, 'red-crayon-ness', rather than 'red-ness'.

On a later occasion, she pointed to a patch of colour in a book and vocalised, 'yellow', or something like that. It seemed like the number of instances in which she would name a colour was increasing, suggesting that the concepts of 'red', 'yellow', etc. were being generalised across different objects and contexts. This process will continue: blue crayons, blue socks, (pale) blue sky, and in time, blue copper sulphate. Science ideas such as temperature, mass, and growth, etc. may start with concrete instances, but must become conceptual abstractions. That is, the colour is abstracted or 'taken out of' the specific instance to become a conceptual generalisation. Concepts are built up over a lifetime through experience of many individual cases, objects and contexts.

Multimodal perspectives on concept development

Classification using set membership activities illustrates the general principle of how science ideas develop. The practical sorting activity may be accompanied by a significant language requirement. Language plays an important role in learning, but other significant modes of expression are also available to children. These must not be overlooked or neglected. They need to be explored productively by educators. Language has a higher level organising role in our interpretation of a modular theory of mind. This makes sense intuitively if we reflect on the experience we all have occasionally: that of not knowing clearly what we think or believe until we speak the thought or write down the idea. The struggle to express what is in our mind is clarified by the act of articulation. That which was internal and on the point of emerging becomes public and explicit. Speaking and listening in a social context helps children to clarify their own thinking through the act of enunciation. It also makes feedback possible, whether or not solicited. While acknowledging the importance of language in dialogic processes, we also wish to emphasise the role of a wide range of other modes of expression and communication. Multimodal experiences enrich and extend conceptual knowledge and can be used singly or in combination (Russell and McGuigan, 2003; Russell, 2015a). They provide the fundamental information we refer to in thinking, speaking, writing and enacting to communicate, as the following paragraphs describe.

Physical manipulation

The role of hands-on activity in cognitive adaptation to the physical environment is the area of research pioneered by Inhelder and Piaget (1964). Their 'concrete operational thinking' refers to the manipulation of real objects as a way of coming to know by doing. The transformations in hands-on activities are physical: shaping, rearranging, pouring, building, balancing, classifying, ordering, and so forth (Shayer and Adey, 1981; Adey, 2008). They are also universal in the sense that they can happen anywhere and everywhere; pouring water can happen from the contents of a puddle, the bath or using a designer trough in a nursery. Learning that various physical dimensions such as number, mass and volume are conserved despite being changed in outward superficial appearance can take place via direct interactions with the material world. These conservations apply to anything and everything: the numbers of either acorns or plastic counters; the mass of either soil or mashed potato; the volume of either mud or modelling clay. The actual content or context is not the critical feature. It is the handling, transforming, observing and direct involvement that constitute the indispensable features that have an impact on intellectual development. Klahr (2012) argues that by 7 years of age, most children distinguish between those transformations that have an effect on the number of items in a set such as removal by eating, and transformations that do not, such as stretching, compressing, etc. The possibility that these cognitive developments can take place through silent, engrossed, solitary activity raises the question of whether they are independent of language. In reality, the transformations of materials are often accompanied by spontaneous commentary, frequently during parallel or co-operative play. There is strong evidence that working in a group can be advantageous for conceptual development. Howe's work with pupils aged 8 and over confirms that 'the more that students discuss contrasting ideas, the more progress they make towards conceptual mastery' (Howe, 2014, p. 109). What is particularly fascinating in Howe's work is the observation that growth in children's learning seems to continue long after the group exchange. It seems that the experience of discordant ideas triggers 'reprocessing' after the event – perhaps at a subliminal level. It is as though our mind-brains continue processing, below the level of conscious control, to resolve discrepancies and that this process results in new learning. This perspective is at odds with the idea of the educator as the overseer of all productive learning events. The inference to be drawn is that putting children together in small groups in which different points of view are exchanged is a productive strategy that does not depend either on teacher oversight or consensus resolution at the time of the discussion. Being exposed to different points of view is in itself productive for conceptual development.

At a more conscious level, language offers opportunities for shoring up hands-on understanding by adding a self-aware metacognitive dimension. This level of re-representation or 'representational redescription' (Karmiloff-Smith, 2012) from actions to words is likely to benefit from interactions which include adult prompting. These interactions can help shape children's behaviours by bringing relevant aspects of their experiences to their awareness.

The early years will offer children hands-on experiences of the classical conservations (number, length, mass, volume, etc.) through explorations that might include bending, stretching, rolling, mixing, squashing, pouring and sieving. These are all reversible transformations. Children will also need to encounter and appreciate irreversible changes. These are likely to be most familiar from cooking, where foodstuff is transformed, usually irreversibly (so that the original material cannot be retrieved). All these directly experienced transformations contribute to children's conceptual understanding of the world of materials. Redescribing directly experienced events using language will help nurture developing understanding.

Background science

Heat and cooking

Children might experience reversible changes through the moderate heating of chocolate or ice, such that the original material remains unchanged other than in shape, and can be changed back to its original form. By contrast, baking cakes causes irreversible changes that can be seen, felt, smelt and tasted. We use heat to break down food to make it digestible. Direct radiant heat at about 200° C is used in barbecues, grilling and broiling, while boiling subjects food to the boiling temperature of water at 100° C.

All these directly experienced transformations contribute to children's conceptual understanding of the world of materials. Redescribing events using language and drawing will consolidate that understanding, but the direct experience is irreplaceable.

Acting and dramatising

Actions, gestures, facial expressions and mime may occasionally be more accessible modes of expression than words. Or they may add nuances that children lack the vocabulary to elaborate, perhaps serving as similes in action. There is accumulating research evidence of the interaction between thinking and whole body movements (Barsalou, 2008) and a burgeoning area of research and practice termed 'embodied cognition'. Use of gesture is thought to change and enhance understandings (Goldin-Meadow, 2009). Our research activities exploring children's science ideas have confirmed how children's understandings that may not be possible to communicate via speech might be readily expressed by using gestures and actions. Ideas may be expressed using drama and movement: the weather (wind, rain, sunshine), animal behaviours and life cycles or plant growth. Dramatisations can be used to represent science concepts such as the properties of some materials with pairs of children acting as magnets while others represent different materials that may or may not be attracted. Understanding of the transformation of frogspawn into tadpoles and frogs might be mimed, with children's own muscles, nerves and body shapes mediating understanding of different facets of the frog's life cycle. We suggest being alert and sensitive to possibilities for exploring spontaneously-arising representational possibilities. Children's gestures are often artless but full of meaning. They can be treated as significant conveyors of meaning rather than incidental twitching or squirming! Imaginative improvisation can relieve dependence on language alone and extend understanding through less conventional, often overlooked, modalities.

Pause for thought

Using whole body movements to communicate ideas

Keira (aged 5) was describing the growth of sycamore seeds. She had noticed that the seeds grew in open areas of the field adjacent to her school, but not under the perimeter trees. She explained that the branches and leaves of the tree prevented rain and sunlight reaching the seeds that landed in the tree's shade. As she spoke, she extended her arms and fingers to represent the branches of the tree; she wiggled the fingers of both hands to convey the falling rain. She uncoiled, stretching her arms and whole body upwards to show the act of the seed germinating and reaching for the light. Her actions were evocative and led to the suggestion of group dramatisations of the conditions for seeds to geminate. Some children would curl up as seeds while others acted as rain or the warmth of sunlight to initiate their growth.

Role-play and 'dressing up' is a familiar early years occupation, stimulated or defined by particular garments and props: a nurse's uniform, a builder's or fire officer's helmet, cooking utensils, and so forth. Each 'prop' has the potential to set a context. Health, hygiene and parts of the body for nurses and patients; materials and the irreversible change of burning for builders and fire officers; appreciation of reversible and irreversible changes used in cooking, as well as measuring quantities, timing, dividing and sharing portions. Adopting a role opens children up to new experiences as they step out of their personal identities into those of other characters. These transformations can also use the proxy of puppets with the virtue that puppeteers must adopt a persona other than their habitual selves. This may liberate children, allowing them to express novel points of view. There is the option for acting out ideas of particular role models, including scientists. ('What might a scientist do in this situation? Shall we let the puppet show us?'.) Using puppets may also facilitate development of a Theory of Mind (Chapter 6), with the appreciation that others have their own minds and ideas that may differ from one's own.

Graphic organisers

A graphic organiser is any visual 2-D mix of words and images that acts as a scaffold to support thinking. Geographic maps set out the spatial relationships between locations and enable distances, routes and journeys to be worked out in advance, often with topographical detail. 'Mind maps' or 'concept maps' (a.k.a 'spider diagrams'), rather than dealing with physical topography, make explicit connections between ideas, using labels on linking lines to add detail. 'Storyboards' are familiar in the film and video industry, where a sequence of picture strip images with annotations summarises the logical flow, contexts and characters, twists and byways in a plot, prior to filming. The term 'road map' extends the analogy of a journey by identifying points in sequence. This representational form has been found exceptionally useful in supporting children's oral presentations, serving as a visual script of the main points to be communicated.

Pause for thought

Road map

In constructing their 'road map' explaining dinosaur extinction, a group of 4 and 5 year olds worked together to produce a linear sequence of ideas. (The number of ideas added is not constrained by the format.)

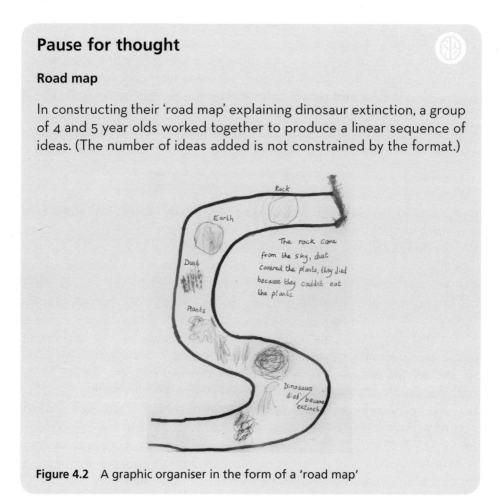

Figure 4.2 A graphic organiser in the form of a 'road map'

The map works from top to bottom of the 'road', with written annotations added to the drawing by an adult in this case, as narrated by
the children. The map explains that a meteor came from space and hit
the Earth, causing dust that covered dinosaurs' food plants, thus causing their extinction. The road map acted as a graphic organiser and
helped the children to express their ideas as causes and effects. It is a
form of scaffolding for thinking that has wide application in science as
well as across the curriculum.

Visual or auditory mnemonics are also associated with prodigious feats of
memorisation; the techniques stretching back to Australian aboriginal song
lines (Klapproth, 2004). In the context of learning science concepts, we are
concerned with the logical organisation of knowledge. All graphic organis-
ers reduce demands on short-term working memory by mapping to an
external 2-D or 3-D visual scaffold. A 3-D example is a (pre-digital) 'memory
stick', a device serving as a record when children make an exploratory
walk through a new environment or habitat. Children capture details of
their journey in sequence and attach mementoes to their stick: soil, leaves,
drawings, words or photographs. These graphic recording stratagems are
invaluable to children's reporting back to their peers of past and present
episodes, situations or experiences. They add further possibilities for transforming and internalising experiences into coherently organised conceptual
understanding of science-related objects and events.

Drawing as transformation of visual observation

The earliest human 2-D representations available to us today date from
about 40,000 years ago in the form of cave paintings located in Spain and
Indonesia. Mark making has a tremendously important role in human activity that might begin in present-day children with marks made with a stick
in sand, a finger in condensation on a windowpane, footprints in mud or
hands in foam. Drawings are an external notation using any medium: pen-
cils, crayons, sticks, sponges, brushes, any implement applied to a 2-D
surface to leave marks, permanent or ephemeral. This inclination to represent ideas in 2-D is exploited by educators as an early approach to
recording numerals, letters and words as well as images.

The act of seeing must include sense making. It demands 'brains on' as
well as eyes open. To be meaningful, visual perception requires mental
transformation. A close observation of detail will enable an object, event or
person to be noted, remembered and understood better. Drawn recordings

can play an important role in this assimilation process. Drawing involves a transformation of perception, a re-representation of what is seen from one visual form (real life 3-D) to another (2-D image). The process of drawing requires scrutiny to be intense, with great attention to detail and reflection on and selection of the salient features to record. Complementing the act of drawing as a process is the product, the image, which can be returned to as an external memorisation of the object. The process and product of drawing result in a better-informed understanding of the concept represented, whether a leaf, a fossil, tree, rock, insect, burning candle or slice of bread.

Drawing with a more decorative or imaginative intention in mind is also explored for its value in encouraging fine motor control. Exploratory mark making can be a direct stimulus for extending the vocabulary of shape, colour and texture, as well as the imaginative vehicle for expression of emotional or narrative ideas.

Distinction between imaginative and observational drawing

Children's early drawings may be motivated by imaginative expression rather than any attempt at recording aspects of the real world and often have a raw freshness and communicative appeal in their innocence and 'artlessness'. They may also be influenced by stereotypes, due to the fact that the ways of representing objects in 2-D with which they are surrounded soon become familiar from various media. For example, the Sun, the Moon and stars in the sky will have a conventional and formulaic mode of being illustrated. They may also reveal some ideas about cosmology, including the idea that clouds around the Sun cause nightfall. Drawn clouds may be stereotypical, suggesting that an adult's guidance to invite children to glance at how clouds 'really' appear would be opportune.

Pause for thought

Drawing and observation

Children's drawings of flying birds may defy the laws of physics. The way the trees have been drawn in the illustration in Figure 4.3 is more stylistically conforming than accurate, illustrating how socialisation can shape the way children represent (and perhaps even the way they see) the world. The 5-year old's drawing of the chicken includes observational detail in the beak, comb, wings and tail, though with a surprising discrepancy in the set

of four legs. This divergence between the representation and the represented may be the result of a lapse of concentration that could be
corrected readily, once pointed out. It is also a fact that young children
typically characterise animals as having four legs. It seems very likely that
the chicken has been drawn in the absence of any feedback between the
subject (a chicken) and the drawn representation. Looking back and forth
between object and drawing is the critical component of observational
drawing and is a skill that needs to be taught and learned.

Figure 4.3   Does the drawing use observation, imagination or convention?

Children's representations of the way they understand the world are of
particular interest in what they reveal about their thinking. Their drawings
of real things, what we term 'observational drawings' (as contrasted with
imaginative drawings) are significant in the context of their emergent science behaviours. Drawings from observation have had an important role
in the development of science. Galileo (1564–1642) used the newly
invented optical telescope to observe and record systematically in drawings
of the Moon, Jupiter and the Milky Way, confirming the heliocentric solar
system. Trained artists recorded the new species, topographies and cus-
toms of the peoples encountered during the expeditions of Captain James
Cook (1728–79) and of Charles Darwin (1809–82) on the Beagle.

While imaginative drawing is also valued for its role in children's development, observational drawings require the closer attention to truth,
accuracy and detail that are characteristic of scientific behaviour. Observation
of form, texture, shape and proportion are essential elements. Adults play
an important role in encouraging more focused observation as children

iterate between object and drawing. Their drawn marks selectively map features of the drawn object and can be read as a conscious interpretation of what they have perceived. As the chicken illustration confirms, there are many opportunities for slippage between direct perception and mark making. Observational drawing requires close attention to the image on the retina and care taken to represent what is seen rather than what is known. The fact that what people believe influences what they see is an important consideration in science education, where the intention is to establish agreement as to what is factually correct.

The kind of drawing produced by a 4 year old (Figure 4.4) of a small insect that emerged from some fallen leaves is an example of 'theory laden perception' in the sense that the drawing reveals what the child expects, rather than what is actually visible.

Figure 4.4   An observational drawing strongly influenced by anthropomorphism

Why did this boy draw the insect (aphid) with a face, hands and fingers, and when asked, 'Is that exactly the same as the insect you have there?' confirm, 'Yes, exactly the same'? The interpretation is that he drew what he *believed* he could see. His visual input was being filtered by his beliefs. Book illustrations aimed at children make frequent and deliberate use of anthropomorphism, giving objects and animals human attributes. The boy may also have had a belief that the aphid has eyes and limbs, and that he could identify these. (We have also to bear in mind that the visual acuity of young children is likely to be very much sharper than that of the adults teaching them.

This aphid was no more than 1.5mm in length.) Perhaps then he resorted to a familiar drawing stereotype to represent features he was aware were present and he truly believed he had drawn what he had seen.

Using multiple sources: composite observational drawings

It is not always possible for children to have access to a static and captive object as the subject of their observational drawing. They may need to refer to available images from various sources to build a picture of the features that interest them, in which case examining several versions of the same target object can be a useful strategy. The alternative sources, in addition to photographs, might include video and 3-D models, even soft toys. Using all these sources is a form of research whereby partial information can be abstracted into a new, amalgamated representation. This is exactly the kind of strategy that scientists use, for example, when palae-ontologists assemble a likeness of an extinct species when only fragments of fossils from different locations are available.

Drawn assemblages as a group activity

Drawing and painting usually happen as solo activities, but constructing pictures as an ensemble pursuit opens possibilities for co-operation, taking turns perhaps, and better still, active collaboration. Teamwork necessitates discussion, implying that ideas have to be made explicit by being articu-lated clearly. Large formats of wall or floor drawings as well as relatively small products can all work well, assembled by pairs or small groups. Building these more complex representations benefits from discussion, negotiation and revision of ideas.

Pause for thought

Group compositions

Some children aged 5 years who were researching animals had selected the mole as their subject. They found out as much about moles as possible and made drawings to summarise their information, individually

(Continued)

(Continued)

and in small groups. The image illustrated involved children in almost constant dialogue, commentating as they drew, bouncing ideas off one another, occasionally correcting, approving or contradicting one another in lively, positive exchanges.

Figure 4.5   A small group drawing to build collective understanding

Their teacher offered occasional points to spur them to further thinking and elaboration of their drawing. Their description included the following comment:

> It's a mole tunnel with a big molehill on top. There's a mole on top of it holding a worm and a mouse. There's a nest and there are mole babies (shown in a chamber, lower right) and there's where they keep the food (lower left chamber).

Some details have explanatory labels written against them, a reminder that drawings can be annotated to clarify aspects of what has been drawn or what is happening. Explanatory comments may be added either by the children if they are able to do so, or by an adult to whom the children explain and dictate their intentions. It is important to the conceptual development intent of the activity that the children retain a sense of ownership of the drawing and its informational content.

Background science

Herbivores and carnivores

Animals can be classified according to their diet. Although moles are mostly insectivorous (insect eaters), small mammals may also form part of the mole's diet, so they are also carnivores. Herbivores eat plants only, while omnivores, such as humans, eat anything! Animals' diets can be inferred by looking at their dentition.

Modelling in 3-D

There are many situations in which scientists need to mentally transform 2-D information into a 3-D appreciation of a concept. A common example is the X-ray image. A celebrated one-off event in the history of science was the interpretation of the structure of the DNA molecule as having the form of a double helix (Watson, 1999). An assortment of materials is often reused by children in early years' environments to create, for example, 3-D models of various animals and plants. Models of insects might be constructed, following a simple template of three body parts (head, thorax and abdomen), a pair of antennae, a pair of wings and six pairs of legs attached to the thorax.

New technologies offer children the exciting capability to add gesture-controlled movement to their 3-D models. In one innovative example, children create their model robot, animal, car or whatever by attaching readily available surplus materials (card, paper, etc.) to plastic joints bearing wireless receptors. The parts are attached to the joints using simple hook and loop fastenings. Children then animate their model via hand and finger movements while wearing a 'magic glove'. Those movements are transmitted to the model wirelessly, enabling children to move the model and its parts at a distance in any way they like (Seehra et al., 2015). Innovations of this kind add an extra dimension to the representational potential of children's constructions, helping them to realise a much more diverse range of functionality than is possible with static assemblages.

As with drawing, modelling in 3-D proceeds by iterating between the object (or a substitute image) and its representation, scrutinising and making decisions based on judgements of salience. These processes bolster internalisation of the important attributes and facilitate conceptual understanding of, for example, recurring patterns in the different features of plants and animals.

Sketching ideas rather than objects

Scientific drawings can be imaginative as well as observational, serving to push an individual's limits of comprehension. In like manner, a drawing can crystalize a child's idea or explanation of a phenomenon, as in a drawing of the notion of how sound travels. A sketch is a useful device for trying out an idea in graphical form and is a useful ploy for helping a child to explain their point of view. Forces on moving toys and transfers of energy are unseen, but children are nonetheless making sense of such playful experiences and can make drawings to help show their thinking: what causes objects to move; how they see objects and how they hear (perhaps using some of the lines or arrows they have noticed in books, comics and video to stand for light or sound travelling); what happens when water 'disappears' or evaporates from a cup; the changes inside an incubating egg or a germinating seed. Although such invitations may be considered a challenge for adults, youngsters can be totally unfazed by requests to draw their ideas as 'sketches', implying a looser, less factually precise representation. Describing the intention as to produce 'a rough sketch', to be executed freehand with no attempt at a perfect result, also takes the pressure off those who are apprehensive about committing themselves when they feel unsure of their ideas. Drawn changes of mind and corrections can be left in place and tolerated in a sketch and open up opportunities for discussion and feedback.

Pause for thought

Drawing back through time

As part of a topic on 'animals', the class explored fossils. Marissa (aged 6) drew her understanding of how the fossil came to be.

Figure 4.6 Using a picture strip sequence to show how fossils form over time

The four sections of the picture strip intuitively helped her think about some of the changes by scaffolding the passage of time. She started way back in time with the living animal and where it lived and worked towards present time to show how the animal might have changed into a fossil. She explained one of the critical steps: 'Someone put the animal on the rock and it must have sunk in the rock', revealing the common difficulty children have in conceptualising how living materials can turn into fossil 'rock' or 'stone'.

Drawing events that occur over time, either looking back historically or into the future, is made possible by using picture strip conventions. Children become aware of the relevant conventions used to show the passage of time soon after being introduced to picture and story books. The conventions of the direction in which pages are turned as well as the left to right and top to bottom sequence in which images (and later, words) must be tracked are soon learned with the support of adult modelling. These directional assumptions become deeply ingrained to the extent that they feel innate, and all images tend to be 'read' from left to right.

Reflection

With one or more partners if possible, select a science idea to explore with children multimodally, using as many different and varied modes as you can think of. Consider how you might encourage the elicitation of children's ideas and translations from one mode to another.

Summary

This chapter has explored how multimodal approaches support the ways in which children construct and communicate understandings. It is argued that encouraging children's engagement with a variety of modes such as drawing, images, 3-D modelling, writing, speech, movement, number, music, etc. enables meaning making and extends conceptual understanding.

- The discussion of conceptual development in this chapter accented the possibilities for the multimodal expression of ideas available to children and their educators.
- For clarity, different modes have been presented separately. In practice, such separation is unlikely and different modes of expression are more likely to be used interchangeably or together.
- Translation between representations is a key element in conceptual development and something to be encouraged at every opportunity.
- We do not prioritise any particular mode of expression over any other, but emphasise re-representing across and between modes to construct and reveal different aspects of understanding.

5

Working scientifically and developing science enquiry skills

Chapter overview

This chapter discusses emergent science from a 'process' perspective, that is, the skills underpinning 'doing science'. We examine the behaviours that are precursors to children being able to engage in more purposeful and structured enquiries. The general developmental skills of classifying, ordering, observing and pattern seeking are described, as is the curiosity-driven exploration that can develop from playful inquisitiveness into questions that can be investigated using 'fair testing'. This chapter is concerned with investigations using direct experiences.

Explorations, enquiries, investigations 'fair tests' and experiments

Some definitions will offer a useful start to this chapter, so as to ensure clarity about what we expect of children and in what direction educators might aspire to lead them. The broad subject addressed is that of 'working scientifically'. Under this umbrella term, an important distinction is between activities that involve *direct experiences* of phenomena and those that depend on accessing *secondary sources* of information. In the public imagination, scientists' activities are more likely to be associated with the former: making observations and measurements of real things, otherwise known as 'empirical studies'. Actually, data gathering from libraries and 'meta-analyses' that overview the published findings of others is an alternative and valid way of working scientifically. In similar fashion, so are children's own library and internet searches that are designed to 'find out' in some way. This chapter will focus on 'finding out' activities via direct experiences.

So as to maintain the developmental perspective this book has adopted throughout, we will begin with the term 'exploration'. There would be no science without inquisitiveness, curiosity and a desire to discover why things are as they are, or work as they do. Exploration involves thinking in action, looking at things from 360°, examining them, perhaps prodding, maybe even dissecting. There is likely to be a question in mind, a purpose that motivates the initial interest: 'What is it? What does it do? Is it alive? Is it dangerous? Is it very rare or precious? What makes it behave the way it does?'. Not infrequently, each answer obtained raises another query. So we are using 'exploration' in the sense of informal, often spontaneous, quite probably unstructured behaviour motivated by the appetite to find out more. Exploration is a key characteristic of effective learning and may be casual, playful, desultory or compulsively enthusiastic. In any particular context, it might last a matter of seconds, hours, days or weeks. In some instances, a chance discovery might ignite a lifetime's passion, as did Richard Fortey's youthful encounter with fossil trilobites. Writing about an early field trip Fortey (1998) captures the mood of how we think of scientific exploration in the youngest of learners through to mature scientists:

> There seemed nothing to interfere with the joy of observation, no end to knowledge, no possibility that any discovery should be less than astounding.
> (Fortey, 1998, p. 2)

That is the joy, the unrestricted excitement of being let loose to explore a world composed of novel objects and events to observe and reflect upon. Science educators value early years' children's exploratory behaviour enormously and try to elicit, sustain and develop it at every opportunity. It confirms that children are thinking, interested and want to know more.

Pause for thought

Science process and concept interaction

A 3 year old had found a sycamore seed (known colloquially as 'helicopters' due to their wings and spiralling manner of flight) and after observing it closely began to collect more of the seeds. Building on the child's interest, the teacher pointed out to a group of children how the seeds were scattered around the trunk of the sycamore tree. Their discussion turned one child's curiosity for seed collecting into an experience that engaged the group of 3 to 5 year olds. In pairs, children set off from the tree to look in the grass for more sycamore seeds. To show where they found a seed they agreed to put a home-made flag in the ground. Counting the number of foot-steps to the seed added a measurement dimension to the exploration. A competition developed amongst some of the children to find the seed the furthest away from the tree. The pair in Figure 5.1 has found a seed, one child marking the position with her foot while the other places the flag in the ground to record the seed's location. Those children who had managed to count footsteps recorded the number of steps away from the parent tree on the flag – often with an adult's help. Reviewing all the flags, children noticed with their teacher's help the pattern of more flags closer to the tree and fewer further away. This led to a discussion of possible reasons and how some seeds had managed to travel so far. This is an excellent example of the potential of working scientifically (pattern recognition) to interact with conceptual understanding (the forces causing seed distribution) to enhance understanding.

Figure 5.1   Flagging the position of sycamore seeds

Another word strongly associated with children working scientifically is 'enquiry' – having the everyday sense of actively questioning and seeking answers, either from secondary sources or via direct experiences. We are concerned with the latter sense at this point in the discussion. Enquiries might be exploratory, but can be thought of as more persistent, structured, slightly more formal and more explicit than the way in which we have characterised exploration. Another term used, seemingly synonymously with 'enquiry', is 'investigation'. Both of these behaviours are associated with purposeful activity, more focused than the open-endedness of an exploration, though the latter might well develop into a more purposeful enquiry or investigation. This is especially likely when educators recognise children's interest and build on that sign of motivation by showing attentiveness and encouraging discussion. Adults can help the child to reformulate a generalised interest into a more focused question and a more systematic effort to collect information. This is how science learning can develop from the germ of curiosity into evidence-based expert knowledge.

A term that has been adopted to meet the needs of working scientifically in the early years phase of education is the 'fair test'. It describes an early form of enquiry in which children's more general awareness of what is fair – in sharing, taking turns, apportioning treats, and so forth – is brought to bear on comparisons in a science context. It is a well-established science procedure in the early years, appealing as it does to children's sense of justice and their sensitivity to being treated equably. The development of an understanding of fair testing owes much to socio-cultural expectations and the sense of fairness that is instilled and regulated by carers and parents. For a test to be fair, children must consider what circumstances, conditions or 'factors' (also known as 'variables') in an enquiry would need to be kept the same, or 'controlled'. Comparisons that are part of their enquiry must avoid the possibility of being 'unfair', or as they will later understand, being 'invalid'. Everyday examples of what is fair and what is not will be very familiar to children (Turner et al., 2011). In a running race, even the youngest children appreciate that the starting time and place, distance to be covered, the running surface and finish line must be the same for all participants. (They might try to 'steal a march' on fellow competitors, but they will know exactly what advantage they are trying to gain and so will their peers!) If they were measuring one another's height, most would soon recognise that it would be unfair if some children stretched while others slumped, or if there were to be a mix of tiptoes, wearing shoes or going barefoot. Children become so adept at fair testing that the 'control everything' syndrome commonly emerges. That is, children will suggest controls that are not relevant: that the same person must play the same role, perhaps even wearing the same clothing. An adult posing the question, 'Do you think that will make a difference to our results?' is a useful prompt in those circumstances. However, adults are not immune from carrying fair testing into adulthood in the form of superstitions: sports people who feel the need to follow obsessive rituals of dress or behaviour to ensure optimal performance are commonplace.

While explorations, fair tests, enquiries and investigations might all be expected to be seen and promoted in the early years, an 'experiment' introduces a term more familiar to secondary science, though some primary educators like to use it. It implies a more formal procedure using apparatus and measurement, often conducted under laboratory or field research conditions, though not invariably so. Einstein was famous for having conducted 'mind experiments', working through scenarios using imaginative vision, creativity and inventiveness, a reminder that these attributes are as important in the STEM subjects as to the arts.

Science process skills

Another way of thinking about working scientifically, whether in the early years or through primary education and beyond, is to analyse the skills involved – the 'science process skills'. An enormous volume of international research and development work has been conducted in this area, often through large-scale national projects (see, for example, the work of the Assessment of Performance Unit; DES, 1985). Although less attention has been paid to the science process skills as deployed in the early years, the fundamentals are common to any age group and recognisable in their essential nature, though differing in the quality, proficiency or insight with which they are deployed. Consensus in listing these science process skills is not difficult, give or take minor differences. We might begin with *observing*, a skill closely connected to *measuring* in the sense that the latter permits observations to be pegged to a quantitative scale: size, mass, volume, and so forth. Enquiries require a beginning, an end and something happening in the middle, so science *planning* is another skill to be learned and called upon. They also entail expectations about outcomes, however uncertain they may be and these take the form of *predicting* (on the basis of a pattern in data) or *hypothesising* (informed by a conceptual understanding or theory of why something happens the way it does). If there is a practical element requiring the use of apparatus or measuring instruments, the skills of *using apparatus* will need to be called upon. The results will need *recording* in some manner (using lists, tables, bar charts, or graphs, as appropriate). Likewise, other people's data require *data reading* skills, and not least, whether one's own or somebody else's, *interpreting* or discerning patterns in the results. Some frameworks include *applying science knowledge and understanding* (for example, APU, DES op. cit.) as a science process skill.

Attempting to teach all the discrete science process skills itemised separately above is not a valid proposition, though it would be legitimate to reflect back to children what skills they are using in real time, as they happen. To deal with individual skills out of context would risk leaving them devoid of purpose when their main function is to support understanding of the subject matter of an enquiry. However, it *is* possible and desirable to encourage children to engage in clusters of skills that form meaningful and purposeful sub-routines. This possibility is reinforced by the fact that the skills almost invariably are called upon in clusters: observing, measuring and interpreting patterns, for example. As will be illustrated, some sub-routines can be regarded as complete enquiries in themselves, rather than as an approximation to a full investigation.

Working scientifically: using a 'research meeting' procedure

Early years practice should include many examples of children being encouraged to collaborate to bring about shared outcomes. This approach is important because it models for children the growth of science knowledge as a social process. Exchanging ideas can serve to provide insights into others' perspectives on enquiries that arise as the result of discussion. We encourage the use of a structured framework to guide the process of these collaborative science enquiries. Children's own research can be pooled, presented and debated through a process referred to as a 'research meeting'. This term (coined by Lehrer and Schauble, 2012) is introduced to children so that the act of behaving as scientists is a conscious one for them. Children can then distinguish research meetings from other forms of discussion: they can learn the rules of the procedure and adopt the roles of 'presenter' and 'listener', as required. With this structure in mind, research meetings can be planned for and nurtured in the early years environment.

Educators necessarily play an important role in fostering the gradual emergence of these skills in the questions they pose to encourage critical feedback and attentive listening. The key aspects of the research meeting are as follows.

Children *presenting* must:

- describe their research question, e.g. starting ideas or question(s) that stimulated their research enquiry
- explain what they have found out so far, i.e. present their ideas or 'claims'
- back up their claims with evidence, i.e. present evidence, describe sources
- share any uncertainties, e.g. gaps in knowledge, failures to find information or evidence
- ask for support from their peers, e.g. to resolve conflicting or confusing information.

Children *actively listening* must:

- reflect on what they have heard and learned from the presenter(s) in the light of their own ideas, i.e. review their own beliefs in order to make sense of someone else's point of view
- make responsive suggestions on the basis of what they have heard and what they know, e.g. offer new ideas, new lines of enquiry, etc.
- raise questions to clarify or challenge the ideas.

For the very youngest children who are least experienced with the requirements, when acting as presenter, simply expressing one of their own ideas to the group is a good beginning. The role of active listener can be confirmed very modestly initially, just by paying attention and repeating back the ideas expressed by others. These simple acts will comprise a satisfying beginning.

Classifying and ordering

Classifying and ordering are less science-specific skills than part of general intellectual development. They are fundamental to what are called 'logico-mathematical' skills and therefore underpin all intellectual development relevant to STEM subjects. For example, the number system combines ordinal and cardinal properties: objects can be classified into sets of five sweets, five beads, five stones, and so on, to establish 'five-ness' as a quality of a set unrestricted by the kind of object. Those sets can then be placed in order, becoming smaller or larger. Classifying has more obvious science relevance when the objects or events to be classified refer to the subject matter content of science. (The concept of 'alive', for example, is obviously relevant to biology and is discussed in Chapter 4.) Classifying is relevant to very young children as they determine the critical attributes that determine set membership for many different kinds of descriptive labels: colour, mass, length, transparency, and so on. Although classifying can be engaged in at a simple level, it can also continue to limitless levels of sophistication and complexity, as with physicists' ongoing struggle with the classification of the fundamental particles that constitute matter.

Pause for thought

Classifying by blowing

A fictional story, *The Windy Day* (Milbourne, 2012), provided a context and the starting point for the study of wind and the effects of its force. The story prompted a group of 4 year olds to review what they knew about windy weather, what sort of materials and objects might be moved by the wind and how, by blowing, they might re-create some of its effects. They were given a straw to blow through and set off in all directions to explore the effects of blowing objects, including their teacher's hair! The teacher's questions during their explorations persuaded them not just to blow, but also to observe the effect of blowing on each object's movement and shape and to notice any incidental sounds: 'Can you see anything happening? What happened? Why do you think that happened?'. Some of the teacher's questions encouraged children to vary the force of their blowing: 'What happens to the paper when you blow really hard? Can you try a really gentle blow? What do you see happening?'.

Their teacher guided them towards a more systematic enquiry into the effects of blowing by providing pairs of children with some of the objects they had blown randomly. She then asked them to sort the objects into two sets using hoops as set boundaries, one labelled, 'Things that moved' when blown, the other, 'Things that did not move'.

Figure 5.2   Exploring things that move or stay still when blown

Observation and classification combined as described add a degree of structure and focus to extend children's initial explorations. The activity aimed to help children to test and observe each object in turn. Putting the objects into groups provided a physical, albeit temporary, record of the outcome of their enquiry that they could review to discover common attributes of the members of each set. Classification experiences of this kind are strongly linked to building up understanding of scientific terms. They might cohere as stand-alone enquiries, and in some instances, classifying activities may form the basis for using fair tests in more controlled investigations.

From direct experiences to formulating enquiries

As described in Chapter 2, data derived from our work on a 'whole child' observation schedule provided a large volume of information on aspects of behaviour spanning the whole early years phase. By reviewing the entire gamut of behaviours it was possible to identify from the holistic practices of early years practitioners three clusters of activity relevant to emergent science (Russell and McGuigan, 2016). Here, we will revisit the precursors of science enquiry skills.

Curiosity, exploration and raising questions

An appropriate starting point for the journey into science enquiry can be identified in the activities that are a key element in early years provision: the commonly planned opportunities for children to engage in direct experiences. The nuances of this position are often misunderstood by the public at large and may be caricatured negatively as 'leaving children to their own devices'. Allowing children the freedom to reveal their own motivation is positive, provided adults are alert and sensitive to the signals and are available to nurture those interests in constructive directions.

Particular equipment and materials are typically made available in settings – a water trough, sand tray, role-play area with dressing up materials, costumes, and so forth. This provision is designed to promote physical exploration. Thinking about these activities from a science education focus raises the question as to how it might be possible to maximize the value and extend these exploratory experiences, with a view to laying the foundations of later, more structured approaches to science enquiry. The availability of particular resources self-evidently increases the probability of behaviours related to those materials: estimating and measuring time and volume in the outdoor kitchen; building structures, joining pipes, moving water and sand in the building area, etc. Additional, spontaneous or seasonal activities can be accessible to even the youngest children, such as observational walks in the local environment. Typical unplanned events that captivate children include playing with the ice that forms on the water in an outdoor trough, or autumn leaves falling in the play area. Such happenings engage youngsters' attention, provoke curiosity and promote the physical manipulation of materials that we characterise as exploratory. These playful explorations support personal and social development through the exchanges they stimulate; they facilitate vocabulary development because children comment on their discoveries and exchange views about what they are experiencing and generally extend knowledge and understanding of the world.

In order to gain insights into children's views of some of these exploratory activities, we conducted informal interviews, using small groups so that they remained perfectly at ease. The children were familiar with us as the result of several visits to their class and care was taken to make them feel comfortable, to have the concrete materials to which they might wish to refer present and to work with the more outgoing children who volunteered themselves when offered the opportunity to 'tell the visitors' about what they had been doing. A striking outcome was how little children were able (or saw fit) to say about the experiences with which they had been engaged. In the younger age range, children's vocabulary and ability to describe activities can be expected to be limited to brief phrases. It is tempting in the face of minimal responses to assume that children have more understanding than they are able to articulate. Certainly, limited language and vocabulary might be attributable to less privileged social backgrounds and would be the responsible educators' priority for attention. In common with the activity theorists (Plakitsi, 2013), we accepted the primacy of experience in language development; first comes the sensation of the event, emotion or object, and then the words can be attached. We feel the need to add a psychological dimension that the activity theorists eschew as 'mentalistic'. Our theoretical sense was that children needed to transform their physical experiences, to re-represent them mentally and linguistically in the process described as 'representational redescription' or 'RR' (Karmiloff-Smith, 2012). It seemed to us that this metacognitive act, which can undoubtedly be promoted by adult involvement and may even depend on it, is easily overlooked in the hurly-burly of settings' activities.

In the context of the multitude of stimuli that early years settings offer, many events are short-lived and children have to be receptive to cues to work out which activities adults regard as important. If adults deem it desirable for children to reflect on their experiences, that expectation must be brought to children's awareness. The providing adults must be clear about what they want children to gain from what is provided for them. Sometimes, expectations are planned and self-evident because they are in-built, as for example, the use of a water trough with jugs, funnels and different shaped vessels. Then, the value may be planned and rehearsed (to some extent but never totally) and adults can be prepared with their responses and cues. At other times, as when an event or interest arises unexpectedly, the situation requires adults to think on their feet. The common factor must be for the adults to be asking themselves, 'What potential added value for the children can we envisage in this scenario?' and 'How do we frame our interactions to optimise positive outcomes?'. Questioning stimulates children to reflect on how they might vary what they are doing and the cause and effect relationships they are experiencing. Children might then become more aware of some of their actions that might otherwise pass in an ephemeral, non-reflective manner.

Pause for thought

Explorations with bubbles

Some 5–6 year old children had been outside on a chill, blustery day, using wire frames and soap mixture in a trough to make bubbles. The wind was strong enough to cause bubbles to form and soar away over the roof tops. There was no need for the children to blow, provided they held their bubble frames at right angles to the direction of the wind. They were impervious to the cold, excited and engaged at the occasional large, long-lasting bubbles. Back indoors, when invited to describe how they made a bubble, the typical response was, 'You blow', which was not actually what had happened. It was as though an enjoyable event had happened, given them pleasure and was in the past, so they felt there was little to discuss. These children did not lack language or ability. There was a discrepancy between the expectations implicit in the questions posed, and the assumptions of the children responding. In science, observation implies poring over things carefully and if necessary, repeatedly, to extract meaning in something like a slow motion replay effect. These children's reference seemed more closely related to their life worlds, where experiences are enjoyed as they happen in the here and now. Then they move on to the next activity. They seemed not to recognise the possibility of reflecting on what they had enjoyed, questioning why things happened in the way they did such that they might increase their success rate in bubble production. The success rate in immersing the frame, lifting it to face the wind and generating a large bubble was actually rather poor – less than 20% – and invited the question that remained unasked, 'What is the most successful way to make a bubble?'.

In order for the bubble blowing or any other activity to become a source of question raising, children would need to reflect on what was happening and wonder why. The musing might happen in dialogue with other children, with adults, or reflectively. Looking further ahead, to be productive as a fair test, bubble production would need to be thought about in terms of its component elements or variable factors. The shape of the bubble frame, the way it was held and immersed, the quality of the soap mixture, the angle the frame was held to the wind or blown – all of these 'factors' would be encouraged to be thought about through discussion and stimulated by the questions posed by an adult. Then children could become aware of the detail, the factors that might be affecting the outcome so that they could modify their tools or technique to control the consequences. At that point, with a clear signal from adults as to the framework they were working within, children would be able to move from experience and observation to a simple form of enquiry. With adult support for the child's expressed interest, it will be possible to sustain children in framing a question capable of being subjected to some form of test or enquiry: an 'investigable question'. This is something that is difficult for young children. It will only emerge with support, experience and practice. The provision of direct hands-on experiences can only ever be a starting point for learning to occur; value is added by the interactions between children and adults that build on those starting points.

Reflection

Consider a direct experience that a group of children are involved in. How might you frame open questions that stimulate their curiosity to raise their own questions to investigate further? What kind of dialogue between you and the children might help them to move their thinking in the direction of a simple enquiry that stems from their own ideas?

The role of metacognition in framing questions that can be investigated

Our research into children's experiential activities and the sense they make of them stimulated a productive dialogue between researchers and educators. Specifically, we reflected on how learning progression over four or five years of the early years might be envisaged, from early experiences to learners' own structured enquiries, moving eventually to include quantification. Interviews with younger children identified the necessity for metacognitive reflection as a preliminary to framing questions that could be amenable to practical enquiry. As researchers, we are disposed to deconstruct events, considering each small step in detail prior to reconstructing them, as if in slow motion. The pedagogical challenge was to circumvent the limitations (due to whatever factors) of children's oral expression. Less language-dependent modes were introduced to enable children to relive or re-enact their experiences. Making picture strip sequenced drawings, assembling sequenced photographs of themselves and their peers and using video recording all allowed them to redescribe their experiences. Any of these modes can support children's awareness of events in the correct detailed sequence. The choice of any particular form of representation would need to be suited to the particular enquiry.

Children's 'slow motion' deconstructions can be a way of bridging or facilitating the transition between experience and further enquiry. We see this approach as having general applicability for the minute-by-minute pedagogy employed by adults managing young learners. Conversational interactions between adults and children, supported by external representations (other than language-based), will lead to 'explicitation', or setting out sequences in unambiguous detail. The quality of dialogue between adults and children must create an atmosphere in which children ask *themselves* the reason why things happen in the observed sequence and listen to and critique others' ideas. Adults will be able to encourage this attitude by initiating and modelling questioning behaviours during science-related activities. It is relevant to note that Hoban and Nielsen's (2012) research into 'Slowmation' technique adopts a very similar position (see http://slowmation.com). The 'slow motion animation' technique uses storyboarding and stop frame video recording as a visual narrative to describe a person's or a group's understanding of a concept. It has proved to be a useful technique in the training of teachers to support their science understanding. The Slowmation visual scaffolding is analogous to what we advocate offering children using drawing, picture strip, photographs or video to describe their own understanding.

Another way of supporting the shift from direct experience to investigable questions is to invite children to anticipate the future by rehearsing what they imagine is going to happen in any particular scenario. This invitation to envisage, 'What do you think will happen next?' is used regularly in storytelling sessions but it is equally possible as they explore real-life scenarios. The offer keeps children alert, engaged and curious. From a science education perspective, the procedure can be seen as a precursor to predicting and hypothesising. These two science process skills both may involve conjecture about future events, but are not synonymous. A prediction has more to do with describing sequences of events, causes and effects from established patterns or precedent. Hypotheses call upon science conceptual understanding to explain why something is likely to happen in the future or why it has already happened in the past. Either can be expressed by children in the form of annotated drawings that reveal what they expect is going to happen (e.g. what lies ahead for a block of ice or seeds that have been sown) over a period of time. It is possible for these ideas to be reframed as investigable questions, such as, 'How can we slow down the melting of the ice?' or 'What is the best way to get the seeds to start growing (germinate)?'. Adult support is essential. Direct experiences do not speak for themselves. Managed opportunities to redescribe their experiences in drawings, role-play or using technology can help children to articulate clear steps in a more enquiry-orientated approach. Encouraging children to express their beliefs and reasoning to explain why things happen as they do is an essential part of establishing a science orientation to the world. Incidentally, it is important to recognise that justifying ideas and actions applies equally to adults as to children as a step towards a culture of evidence-based reasoning and empirical enquiry.

Observing

Children's observations might be of static objects or situations; they might be of episodes in which sequential events or changes take place over time. In either case, observation is more likely to be sustained with adult involvement that uses expressions of interest and a suggestion that the event warrants a focus of attention and recording. The observational timescale can be varied from:

- seconds in very brief events (extinguishing a candle flame, blowing a bubble, dissolving a sugar cube, launching a paper aeroplane)
- minutes (a melting ice cube, jelly dissolving, baking biscuits, the movement of clouds)
- hours (a puddle evaporating, a bonfire burning, clothes drying)
- days (seeds germinating)
- weeks (plants growing, eggs incubating and hatching, tadpoles, butterflies or stick insects metamorphosing, birds raising young at a nest box)
- or months (seasonal changes, leaves changing colour and falling from trees, life cycles, the elevation of the Sun in the sky, changes in children's own heights, a compost heap decomposing).

The duration of the observational enquiry and the unit of time used will need to suit both the event being monitored and children's attention span. The latter can be amplified by recording ephemeral events in drawings, paintings, photographs and models. Adult reminders and support will be necessary to prompt younger children's recall of the intention – the question that motivated the observation in the first place. Children can be involved in making decisions about how they make and record their observations, their frequency and number to be recorded.

About 20 observational scenarios have been suggested in the previous paragraph and they are all capable of extending in different directions. Even such a brief list offers boundless possibilities for children's learning about their world through observing what is around them. Different ways of *recording* can also be explored, from examples of the actual objects (e.g. pressed leaves stuck to a chart); traces in the form of prints or paint trails of what has been observed (hand span prints, foot prints, tracks of toy car journeys); drawings or photographs (plant cycles). Eventually, children will arrive at procedures that allow them to quantify outcomes. Initially, non-standard measures can be used (handspans, paces, etc.), gradually introducing standard measures and numbers that represent more abstracted outcomes.

Reflection

Consider a direct experiential activity you are familiar with and which children enjoy. Think about and describe the steps in children's progress based on how that activity might develop. Consider how children might move from exploration to possible enquiries and recording, and comparing (possibly measuring) of results.

Once children have accumulated records of their observations, individually or as a group, the possibility of discerning patterns in their data becomes possible. They may use a pattern to try *predicting* what is likely to happen next. Or they may try *hypothesising* as to why something happens the way it does on the basis of their growing understanding. The possibility of commentary changing from 'A happened, then B', to 'B happened *because* A ...' is also a possibility, signalling a shift to causal reasoning.

Observing variation in living things

There is a widespread view amongst early years children that living things of the same kind (that is, the same species) are all exactly the same, barring minor differences (Gelman and Rhodes, 2012). This is known as 'essentialism', the notion that members of any particular plant or animal species have some essence or uniqueness that makes them identical and is thought to be causally responsible (Keil, 2012) for features or behaviours. It was just such a view that prompted a group of four and five year olds observing black sheep during a farm visit to exclaim, 'They're not sheep! Sheep are white!' (McGuigan and Russell, 2015). In a similar manner, in the context of growing plants, children can think that seeds of the same kind of plant, given the same conditions for growth will turn into plants that all look exactly the same. The fact is that within-species variation is important to understand, because it is what allows evolution to occur. A variation that confers advantage in survival (as in Darwin's 'survival of the fittest') will spread rapidly through a group over repro-ductive generations. So awareness that kinds of animals and plants are not all exactly the same is important. Teachers can use plants in novel ways to help children discover some of the ways that living things of the same kind vary.

In the course of our recent research, children aged 4 and 5 years made drawings of their observations of the sunflower seedlings they had grown. They recorded the number, shape, colour and size of leaves observed. They went on to arrange everyone's seedlings in an ordered line from those having little growth to the tallest seedling. Plants of similar height were then grouped to form columns similar to those in a chart. The line of plants had been transformed into a physical chart to reveal the difference in the heights of the sunflowers. Looking carefully across the plants, children checked that each was in the correct position. They became aware of the possibility of differences between the plants and had embarked on a journey that would lead them to developing skills of measurement, recording and pattern rec-ognition. In terms of conceptual understanding, their awareness of variation in plants and animals of the same kind had been awakened.

Pause for thought

Observation, measurement, recording and pattern recognition

Year 2 children aged 6 and 7 years (Figure 5.3) were exploring differ-ences between bean plants and differences between their hand and foot measurements concurrently. The expectation was that they should make careful observations and measurements and look for pat-terns. Some of the observations and measurements were child-initiated and the teacher introduced others. All measurement possibilities were shared and encouraged, whatever their origin.

All children were encouraged to count the number of leaves growing on their seedlings. Their teacher wanted to raise children's awareness of the variation in the number of leaves on each plant to challenge ideas that all the plants would be the same. The teacher drew a large chart outside onto which children placed their plants. She spotted the 'exag-gerated' counting due to an initial desire of some children to have grown the plant with the most leaves and reminded them to count accurately so

(Continued)

(Continued)

they could trust the results! The plants were placed in columns according to the number of leaves, clearly showing their variation. Children appreciated that there were few plants at each end and a lot in the middle, describing the shape of the distribution as 'like a hill'. Drawing around the outside of the chart helped children become aware of the shape.

Science constantly seeks patterns in information. Representing the results physically using real plants paved the way towards later experiences of representing results in 2-D charts and graphs. Descriptions of the shape as 'hill-shaped' resonates with the bell-shaped normal distribution curve that children will encounter later when they look at patterns of features within groups of living things. Because some aspect of a pattern recurs (that's what makes it a pattern), it allows predictions to be made. The teacher encouraged children's awareness of the recurring hill shape in their measurements of bean growth, handspan and foot length. A further step might be to investigate whether the pattern recurs in other attributes such as children's height, the size of the same kind of fruit, etc.

Figure 5.3   Outlining a 'hill-shaped' curve

Background science

Understanding 'factors' or 'variables'

In any and every enquiry or experiment, something is observed or measured as an outcome; it's called the 'dependent variable'. If we take the question, 'Does talking to tomato plants have any effect on their productivity?', tomato productivity (however we decide to measure it) is our dependent variable. Talking (or not talking) to them is our independent variable.

Before we start our investigation, we need to reflect upon *all* the factors that might have an impact on tomato productivity (soil, fertiliser, watering, temperature, etc.) and select just *one*, and only one, factor as our independent variable. We can then isolate it by keeping everything else constant and observe its effect on tomato productivity. As 'talking to plants' is our chosen independent variable, we need to be clear and precise about the treatment. We could decide on 'talked to' and 'not talked to' as the way we treat our plants. Or we could have a scale, from 'no talk', through a 'little talk', up to 'a lot of talk'. Or we could use different measured time durations of talking. All the other possible effects on tomato production must not be allowed to confound our investigation. We must keep our test 'fair' by keeping those factors the same for every plant – or eliminating them.

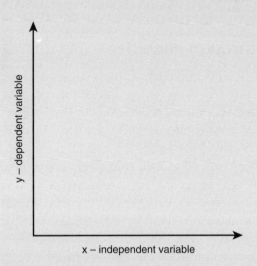

Figure 5.4 A graphical summary of an investigation

(Continued)

(Continued)

Notice that this and most other experiments (certainly all those that will be conducted in primary education) can be summarised graphically in the way shown in Figure 5.4: one factor is changed systematically (the independent variable) to see the effect those changes have on another factor (the dependent variable).

We next run the experiment as planned and check the outcome: tomato productivity. We have further choices to make in our experimental design when we realise we could compare just by observation: 'The plants I talked to look as though they have more tomatoes'. This personal observation might not convince other people. It would be better if we could quantify and measure our results by counting the number of tomatoes per plant, comparing the size of tomatoes or the total mass of tomatoes per plant produced. Once we have our results, we can record and present them in an orderly manner, as a table, bar chart or graph. We can interpret our results by looking for a pattern – and so can anybody else. Of course, others might challenge us if the result is inconclusive or not what they expected. 'Are you sure you used the same tone of voice on every occasion?', 'Was there any sound pollution or extraneous music that could have contaminated your enquiry?', 'Are you sure you made your test fair?'

Progression through enquiries

Children can put objects into sets of things that are the same. In this next example, the set is of toy cars. Toy cars must have similar features of some kind that distinguish them from other kinds of toys. Here, they all have four wheels and can be pushed along. They also vary in some ways.

In this case, as shown in Figure 5.5, the child has made comparisons and observed differences in colour. Two of the cars are blue and two are green. These are put into sub-groups. There are many other features that vary. In science, we refer to these as 'variables' or 'factors'. Enquiries can go quite a long way just by using observation and making comparisons.

If children decide that they wish to compare the distance the cars will travel, they will have to propel them in some way. The child in the case of Figure 5.6 has recorded the outcome in terms of positions of cars at their finishing points. Note the variable is distance travelled, not how fast. The table tells us which of the green cars went further and which of the blue cars went further.

We do not have information to tell us which car, green or blue, travelled furthest of all. A variable that describes the order in which things happen is called
an 'ordinal' variable. A variable that can be matched to a continuously varying
scale is called a 'continuous' variable. When the variable describes groups or
categories, as with colour, it is a 'categorical' variable and it is this form that is
more accessible to children, prior to their acquisition of measurement skills.

Figure 5.5   A labelled drawing as the record of an investigation

Figure 5.6   Adding a grid makes the drawn record more systematic

An important point to notice in the use of the grid is that what is begin-ning to emerge is something like the two-arrow diagram in Figure 5.4. Two factors or variables are being considered in the toy car context: (i) blue or green colour and (ii) relative final position (or distance travelled).

The diagram does not tell us anything about the factors that had to be kept the same in order to make a 'fair test'. Children are adept at identifying how to keep tests fair, or put another way, what variables have to be controlled in order that the enquiry into car colour and finishing position (or distance travelled) produces a reliable result. For example, every car should have the same push or be released in a similar manner from a ramp. The surface over which they travel will certainly make a difference to how far they go, so that will have to be kept the same or 'controlled'. We have to take the cars as given, though their wheels, tyres and axles will all have an effect.

In the next step in progress (as shown in Figure 5.7), the distance differ-ent coloured cars travel (and there are now four colours) is quantified. The children have received adult help by being given lined or squared paper. A non-standard unit of measurement is used to record distance travelled: floor tiles. Provided these are all the same dimensions, they will serve the purpose of comparing distance travelled well.

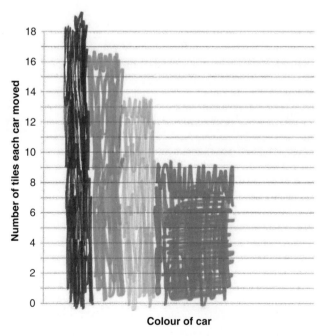

Figure 5.7 A bar chart and labelled axes is a big step forward in recording

We can see from the bar chart (shown in Figure 5.8) which colour of car travelled the greatest distance.

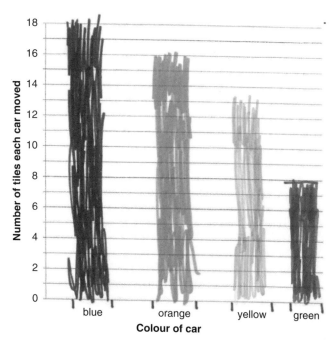

Figure 5.8 Making progress in recording data in bar charts

The shading of the bars is not yet as controlled as it will become. There might also be some growth in the appreciation of the need for accuracy in recording yet to develop. Note that all the numbers in the label of the vertical axis ('Number of tiles each car moved', or dependent variable) are not all in place – only the even numbers. Initially, all the numbers should be in place until children get the hang of labelling axes. As well as the scale being labelled, so is the name of each variable, with 'Colour of car' being the independent variable. The bars are also labelled and as they are not part of a quantified scale, there are no numbers, just the categories of colour.

This bar chart is drawn with more accuracy. Each bar is individually labelled with its colour and is of equal width (approximately). It seems likely that this level of proficiency will soon lead to the measurement of the distance travelled using standard units of measurement, most likely centimetres.

The correspondence with the two-arrow diagram in Figure 5.4 is now more apparent. Incidentally, it is worth mentioning that 'colour of car' is most unlikely to have any effect on distance travelled. However, the nature of such investigations is that each one conducted provokes discussion and reflection and that most certainly is going to be productive, the more so when different points of view are thrown into the mix.

'Fair tests' in the wider context of the 'experimental method'

The 'experimental method' is the pre-eminent mode of working scientifically employed by scientists, translated for school use as children's enquiries or investigations. In adopting an enquiry method, we have to consider the *variability* of whatever we intend to investigate. Take jelly as an example. It varies by wobbliness, flavour, colour, sweetness, transparency and (for older students) its density. All these variable characteristics are 'factors' or 'variables' that describe the nature of any particular jelly. If we are curious to know, 'How long does it take jelly to set?' and decide to find out by using an observational enquiry, we need to be clear what kind of jelly we are working with. This is simply because the kind of jelly is likely to make a difference, so the outcome will vary according to the nature of the jelly we choose to observe. This aspect of investigations, understanding the 'factors' or 'variables' involved in investigating any object or process, is referred to as a 'variable handling' approach. With just a little guidance, children can catch on to the idea of generating as many ways as they can think of in which a named object they intend to be the subject of their enquiry may vary: footwear, apples, fields, shopping bags, balls, water, houses, etc. As a group, they might arrive at the conclusion that apples vary in size, colour, skin texture, hardness, sweetness, number of pips, and so forth. Research has mapped out fairly clearly the logical steps and developmental trajectory children will travel as their understanding increases and their skill in conducting investigations develops. Such 'learning corridors' (Watson et al., 1998; Russell and McGuigan, 2005; Duschl et al., 2007), although extending beyond early years expectations, are useful for practitioners to be aware of because they provide orientation, purpose and direction.

Children's knowledge of working scientifically is best acquired through being involved with engaging real life contexts and subject matter that meets their needs and interests, rather than attempting to work in the abstract. Younger children's observations are likely to be influenced by their interests as well as by adult-initiated activity. As children mature, the curriculum will likely determine the science concepts to be addressed at any given age or year group; enquiry skills may also be partitioned for gradual exposure over time.

The two – process skills and conceptual understanding of subject matter – will interact in complementary fashion, with particular science content being suited to particular modes of enquiry. For example, not all science subject matter lends itself to direct observation, in which case, seeking information from secondary sources of information, including books, videos and photographs from family members, friends or teachers, all offer a preferable research strategy. How evidence gathered from the wide variety of sources available to children might be handled in their discussions is discussed in the next chapter. Nor is it necessary to think of every enquiry as complete in itself, as it is possible to practice sub-routines of enquiry skills or separate elements of an investigation in a stand-alone manner.

Summary

This chapter discussed the manner in which direct experiences will be foundational for the later development of different kinds of enquiry skills.

- Putting children in contact with direct experiences may not be enough - it cannot be assumed that experiences speak for themselves. Encouraging children to redescribe those experiences using other modes such as drawing and speech will help them to develop their understanding.
- There are several different ways in which children can investigate their questions scientifically; the questions or ideas to be investigated will influence the kind of enquiry that is used.
- Some questions might be explored using a number of different types of enquiry and the results considered or reflected upon together as a group. Results and outcomes can then be compared and discussed to support reasoning about different points of view.
- Encouraging children's metacognitive reflection on their enquiries and developing knowledge supports learning and helps children keep track of their progress.
- The development of science process skills can be described fairly readily in terms of gradually accumulating capabilities and the interactions that emerge between the processes of working scientifically and conceptual understanding.

6

Encouraging the expression of ideas

Chapter overview

This chapter discusses children's journey in science from their initial expressions of ideas to rational and reflective critical exchanges between one another. The earliest step involves children revealing and elaborating their ideas in the course of conversations. From this starting point and at their own rate of progress, children can be encouraged to move forward towards discussions in which they share, exchange, reflect upon, critique, debate and challenge ideas and reasoning with one another. The skills acquired in these early science discussions form the foundations of science discourse techniques that are central to what it means to engage in scientific enquiry.

Supporting the development of confidence to express ideas

Developing children's confidence to take an active part in conversations in which they express their thinking and listen and respond to others must be a priority within early years practice. Science activities and the opportunities they provide for children's language development can play a significant supporting role in this priority. Discussing their Preschool Pathways to

Science (PrePS) project, Gelman and Brenneman (2012) describe the need to encourage children's competencies in behaviours such as talk, reasoning and observation in order to help them to develop the tools and capabilities that would position them on relevant pathways towards thinking, talking and working scientifically.

Within early science experiences there needs to be encouragement for children to express themselves confidently and clearly. They should also become aware of the expectation that others' views are to be shown respect by being listened to actively and responded to thoughtfully. With practice they can learn to take account of others' ideas, offer feedback and build on them. Educators will need to adopt particular strategies to support children's expression, justification and thoughtful critique of ideas. The first step is critically important: the encouragement of the expression of their own thoughts. This will represent a considerable challenge for a significant proportion of children entering early years settings.

The skills involved in encouraging young children's participation in conversations, especially those with limited or no background experience of this kind of interaction, should not be underestimated. The expression of the thoughts in their heads requires them to draw upon their developing emotional, linguistic and social skills. Discussions centred on objects that children can handle or a shared experience as it happens in real time, perhaps a story, offer meaningful and engaging starting points. While we acknowledge language to be of primary importance to children's development and achievements, it is just one of a variety of ways in which children might express themselves (Crescenzi et al., 2014).

Drawings, models, actions, role-play and writing can also be valuable communicative modes. Choosing other modes in which children may reveal their understanding is not to circumvent or downplay the importance of language as a pre-eminent means of communication. A multimodal approach emphasises different expressive modes interacting to offer myriad possibilities for conveying meaning. Deliberate attempts at expression using alternative modes will enable children to demonstrate more insights into their thinking than is possible if they were to rely exclusively on language. For instance, aspects of observations about size, sound, relative position and movement of objects might be revealed in drawings, gestures, actions or models that might be impossible to express or would be overlooked in speech. The illustrative examples that follow are consistent with this approach. If children are to offer more than repetition of ideas expressed by others, they must tap into their available productive language, vocabulary and expressive skills to assemble and articulate their own ideas. Even the most limited contribution requires the self-confidence to formulate and articulate what they think. They also need the social opportunities to practice and develop their discussion skills. Our advice is to:

- create an atmosphere in which the expression of all ideas is valued, with judgement on accuracy being reserved or put temporarily on hold
- adopt a conversational style that helps put children at ease and reduces any sense of being confronted or even mildly threatened
- be aware that verbal and non-verbal cues provide the essential social and emotional support for shaping tentative utterances into communications that can be shared and understood by others.

The first steps in engaging in science discussions can be analysed in terms of the following steps:

1. arousing children's awareness of having their own ideas
2. convincing them that their ideas are interesting
3. coming to terms with the fact that it is usual and acceptable for one's own ideas to differ from those of others, and
4. accepting that points of view can be exchanged through debate with other children.

Appreciating that other children have ideas

The expression of ideas involves children making the effort to gain access to their own mental worlds, shifting their consciousness from autopilot to reflective mode in order to access the thoughts inside their heads. As they become confident and active participants in conversations, they begin to assemble their thoughts in a form that enables them to be shared with others. An important feature of these discussions is children's awareness at around 4 years of age that other children have ideas and these may differ from their own. This developing awareness of one's own and other children's minds is significant developmentally and is referred to as an emergent 'theory of mind' (ToM).

Research with young children reveals that we are not born with a sense that others have minds with independent ideas and beliefs. A ToM is a significant emergence in the course of cognitive development, endowing awareness that others have ideas (Baron-Cohen, 1997). Prior to the development of ToM, children assume that whatever they know must be known by everyone as universal facts. To know something is simply to be party to a truth about the world. This way of thinking is referred to as 'realist', because it assumes a world in which there is one reality. That reality is like a video that everyone views and which informs them as to the way things are. There is no sense of the existence of personal, private perspectives. With experience, children come to appreciate that their peers construct their own account of events. While this is a significant step, it is limited in the sense that the beliefs others hold are not regarded as equally acceptable alternatives. Rather, others' ideas are viewed as correct or incorrect, either consistent with the one true reality or not. This treatment of ideas as right or wrong is referred to as an *absolutist* perspective.

After some years of experience and maturation, around the onset of adolescence, a *relativist* capability is seen, in which different points of view are treated as viable alternatives. A more balanced *evaluativist* view is possible only when an internalised value system is established, against which personal judgement can be exercised. This mature way of thinking is unlikely to be in evidence before the age of about 14 years (Kuhn, 2005).

In the context of emergent science in the early years, ToM is an important development. It is vital because exchanging points of view with supporting justifications is a fundamental skill to be developed through science education. Exchanging and evaluating ideas, reasons and evidence is how knowledge is accumulated and validated. Children's journey towards 'argumentation' requires an appreciation that other children have their own minds and points of view.

Background science

Argumentation

'Argumentation' as used in science education refers not to argument in the sense of angry dispute, but as a more formal analysis and description of the exchange of points of view between two or more individuals. An expressed idea is described as a 'claim' and it is the backing of the claim by evidence to justify it that acts as a 'warrant'. Disagreement may be expressed as a 'counter-claim', having its own, different warrant. This same process, but in a more elaborated form, has an exact parallel in scientific research. Researchers make claims supported by evidence that are published in peer-reviewed scientific journals; different or opposing views and evidence are similarly published and so the debate runs according to a set of rules. In a similar manner, children can be helped to engage in rational debate, making claims backed with evidence and listening carefully to different points of view.

Through discourse – serious dialogue or conversation – children become increasingly aware of the range of ideas held by their peers and adults. The importance of the social context and shared activities for children's intellectual development is emphasised by a number of theorists. For instance, Vygotsky (1978) describes understanding as negotiated and built up first in 'the social plane' before being internalised by individuals. The focus of interest for Vygotsky is on development of the individual, albeit with an emphasis on the social context that permits access to expert knowledge drawn from the community.

Another closely related approach inspired by Vygotsky's work is that of activity theory, in which theorists such as Roth (2013), Plakitsi (2013) and Roth et al. (2013) adopt a cultural historical perspective. The critical factor in learning for these science educators is the mutuality of participation in a community endeavour to acquire skills and knowledge. They emphasise that learning involves interactions between participants and the material resources or 'problem space' that is the focus of their activity. Mental tools such as language complement measurement and physical tools such as hand-lenses, rulers and balances. Outcomes are influenced by the implicit and explicit rules that regulate the individual's and group's actions and the distribution of roles and responsibilities across the group. (The stereotype of boys 'doing' while girls watch and record is too familiar in science education.) Cultural historical activity theory frames children's science development in everyday practices across a range of institutions in which the child is involved, including the family and home, the variety of pre-school settings and school. This cluster of theorists regards social learning and collaborative exchanges as critical features of learning science, with learners influencing adults and vice versa.

Practically speaking, early on, educators need to support the expression of what might appear tentative, barely formed or even confused understandings. There is evidence of early emergence of children's curiosity and capability to ask questions to gain information about their experiences of the world. Chouinard (2007) analysed the verbatim transcripts of four children between the ages of 1 year 2 months and 5 years 2 months, collected longitudinally over several years as they interacted with adults. Analysis revealed the surprisingly high number of questions that children asked – an average of 107 questions an hour of which an average of 71 per hour were 'information seeking'. Even when syntactically incomplete the context made clear to the researchers that questions were definitely designed to gain information. Chouinard concluded that limitations in language development may cause children to struggle to find the right way to ask a question but did not affect children's capabilities to attempt to seek information.

The lesson for educators is to be aware of and empathic towards children's struggles to seek information. It is also important to bear in mind that it is the attempt at expression that must be reinforced rather than simply the content of the utterance. Only gradually should there be a shift to require children to express their thoughts clearly and to listen carefully and think about others' ideas. The expectation that all children should make a contribution and have their ideas heeded requires educators to think creatively about how children might be organised and how discussion activities might be managed. Kagan and Kagan (2009) advocate 'structures', essentially grouping and ideas exchanging procedures, for encouraging children's discussion. These are claimed to boost children's confidence and encourage participation and collaborative working. Strategies such as 'timed pair-share' invite pairs of children to take time-limited turns to discuss and share ideas briefly with each other before discussing them more widely with the group or class. The management structure is designed to ensure participation of every child in exchanging ideas. The fact of all children being guaranteed to have their voice heard is designed to boost confidence. In Chapters 3 and 4, we have drawn attention to Howe's work (Howe, 2014) on the importance of children exchanging different points of view for enhancing their learning, so this highly structured technique for ensuring contributions from all participants might be capitalising on that effect.

Adults must play an active role in supporting productive discussions by signalling explicitly that they want children to talk about their ideas while others listen to, think about and respond to what they hear. It will be necessary, during such discourse, to remind children sensitively of these aims, using language and non-verbal cues to urge that all ideas should be treated with respect, with attention paid, effort made to be empathic and interest communicated. It takes time to establish such a culture amongst a group of children and even longer throughout an organisation.

Pause for thought

Exchanging ideas

In the activity illustrated in Figure 6.1, the teacher's aim was to provide children (aged 4 and 5) with a real life direct experience of hens observed at close quarters, which she hoped would excite the expression of ideas. The ground rules for this activity included the teacher reminding children to be sure to describe their ideas and to listen carefully to those of others. The children were excited so needed to be encouraged to be calm and gentle and observe the hens closely using all their senses: to observe (including touching), listen to and

(Continued)

(Continued)

smell the hens. They were asked to observe ways that the hens were the same and ways they were different from one another. Children appreciated that they had their own ideas and were encouraged to add to rather than to repeat what others had said.

Figure 6.1 Sharing children's expressed ideas about chickens

Although some ideas were repeated, a range of observations emerged:

'Ooh, she's orange.'

'She's got big claws.'

'This one is middle-sized.'

'She looks cute. They've all got combs on their heads.'

'She's different colours. They're all different colours.'

'Their beaks are the same.'

'They look the same. This one's actually slimmer and bigger.'

Children's comments showed that they had observed how the hens differed in size and colour and how features such as beaks, combs and claws were common to all. Novel vocabulary was linked directly to the shape, colour, position and movement of the beak or comb, enabling a rich conceptual understanding to be built up. The potential of science activities to support children's developing language was clearly confirmed by their animated discussion. Each child's idea was written down by the teacher and added to the display of photographs with the child's name. In this way, the individual expression of ideas was encouraged and a resource created for children that could enable them to continue to talk about and reflect upon their observations of the hens long after the event.

Making available concrete contexts, using real objects, stories, models, writing or pictures will all help children to appreciate that ideas can be accessed, shared, transformed, shuffled, played with, discussed and reflected upon.

Encouraging children to give reasons to justify ideas

A step on from expressing their own ideas and listening to those of others is the capability to engage in discussions in which children give reasons to justify or explain their ideas and in turn, offer and receive reasoned feedback. Such discussions should be deliberately open-ended so as to encourage a range of alternative ideas. This practice is not simply to encourage more than one idea or explanation. The diversity of viewpoints provides early experiences of comparing and evaluating ideas and recognising that ideas differ in various ways, including being more or less believable, favoured, true, etc. There are specific techniques to build on those already introduced that encourage children to explain and justify their ideas and introduce the requirement to back up assertions with reasons.

Early years educators should, as a deliberate strategy, encourage children very early in their development to offer reasons for their ideas, developing an ethos in which 'I don't know' is challenged. This can be with an expression of reassurance about the good ideas expressed previously coupled with optimism about the ideas yet to be expressed. Accepting responses of the ilk, 'Because, I think so', or 'Because it just is' can be met by posing very gentle challenges such as, 'Why do you think so?' or 'How do you know?'. The point is to invite children at every opportunity to give reasons for their ideas. It will be found helpful to encourage the explicit use of words such as, 'Because …?', perhaps left hanging to signal the expectation of a response. This style of interaction also conveys a genuine interest in each individual's point of view and helps to create a culture in which ideas are valued.

Pause for thought

Arguing a case

A class of 6 and 7 year olds was exploring the topic of dinosaurs and children suggested setting up a class museum. The teacher wanted the class to have ownership of their museum and to decide for themselves which objects were to be included. Though initially uncertain about how the museum could be created, the teacher invited children to bring items to exhibit. She asked them to think about why they wanted each particular object in the museum and reminded them to use 'Because ...' to present a good reason for others to vote for their object's inclusion. The variety of objects brought into the school included books, coins, drawings of things children judged to be old and toys such as a teddy that a child had owned since the time she was born.

The children were organised into small groups and urged to generate a persuasive reason that would attract others' votes. Early in the exchanges, children were tempted to say 'because it is old'. Reasoning in terms of the age of objects is sensible, given the museum context, but the teacher felt that some were simply repeating a reason given previously, rather than thinking for themselves. She wanted them to come to appreciate that they had their own reasons that were interesting and valuable and different to those held by other children. Children found a personal contribution was more difficult, but considering the unique attributes of their own choice of object produced more positive results: 'Think about what is special about your object'. She succeeded in eliciting a variety of reasons by patiently posing questions. For example, 'Can you think of a different reason?'. A range of unique reasoning emerged.

Teddy:	'It's old because I've had it when I was born.'
Book:	'Because we want to learn about dinosaurs.'
Fossils:	'I have seen fossils on TV. They are old.'
Model dinosaur:	'Because we learn how big or small a dinosaur is.'
T. rex drawing:	'I think it should be in the museum because it is really fierce. I saw it in a book.'

The session provided a motivating, meaningful as well as accessible and age-appropriate context for children's discussions. The fact of the quality of children's reasoning being subject to the possible reward of inclusion in the museum promoted the incidence of thoughtful and relevant reasons.

Activities in which adults actively encourage an early focus on children suggesting reasons to support an idea and probe the quality of their explanations lay the foundations for the skills relevant to later scientific reasoning and argument. The explicit encouragement of such reasoning as integral components of children's discussions resonates with the work on dialogic teaching of Alexander (2008) and Mercer and Howe (2012). These researchers express concerns about approaches that simply invite children to 'talk' without guidance or that deploy teacher focused 'question–answer–listen' routines rather than more open-ended questioning that inspires thinking and extended responses. They emphasise the active role adults must play in bringing about the particular kinds of interactions in which children are expected to think, reason and justify their ideas. Prompts considered to encourage such thinking include explicitly asking children for reasons for their views and encouraging them to comment on each other's points of view. Mercer (2013), summarising the available evidence, continues to warn against learning environments dominated by teachers using closed questioning strategies. Instead, he suggests teachers should encourage the expression of understanding and misunderstanding, the exchange of views and the provision of opportunities for children to think aloud, ask questions and explore ideas.

Reflection

In the context of an activity you have conducted or planned, what practical steps could be taken to enhance the possibilities of children:

1. expressing their ideas?
2. giving justifications or reasons?
3. actively listening and responding to the ideas of other children?
4. offering constructive criticism to one another?

Encouraging the thoughtful critique of ideas

Arranging discussions in which children are required to reflect upon and critique their own and others' ideas is an important element in helping children to learn from one another. Critiquing, where children review ideas rather than accept them unquestioningly, assists the construction of new understandings and new ways of reasoning. If children are to learn from one another it makes sense for them to respond in ways that treat others' contributions respectfully, as propositions to be reflected upon and examined rather than to be ignored or dismissed out of hand. The ways that children feed back to others cultivates their confidence as communicators and learners. They need to be reminded not only to listen carefully, but also to be friendly, positive, respectful and constructive in the way they confirm their attentiveness. The responsibility is with adults to model an affirmative climate, one that insists on positive exchanges that are integral to the examination of ideas in emergent science contexts. As well as the tone of response, there are particular phrases adults may explicitly encourage children to use such as, 'I like your idea but…', or 'I think your idea is good but …'. These phrases help to establish a positive, safe atmosphere in which children learn to respond critically, but with empathy and sensitivity, avoiding negativity.

Learning co-operatively requires children to have the capability to form an opinion, compare alternatives and make judgements. As a simple way of beginning this process, once ideas are out in the open, children might review them and decide which they think are 'true' and which they think are 'false'. This process often occurs silently inside children's heads as they make up their minds about preferred options. It can be supported as a practical activity by making the process external rather than internal, with the reasoning being explicit rather than tacit. Deciding between true and false has several advantages. It is a simple 'either–or', categorical form of judgement that is not too challenging. It requires everyone involved to participate actively by making a choice. It is the first step in a discursive process that subsequently moves on to consider justifications for decisions and more nuanced decision making.

Pause for thought

Deciding 'true' or 'false'

Some 6 year olds were given different fruits and vegetables to examine and to consider where they were grown. The teacher wrote on sticky labels ideas about places where the vegetables might grow. Children were encouraged to discuss each idea in small groups and attach each label to either the 'true' or 'false' column on a chart. Making 'true' or 'false' decisions in this context involved children in using their developing knowledge of culinary plants to evaluate statements or propositions (or 'claims' as referred to in the context of 'argumentation'). They needed to examine their own beliefs in order to come to a view about whether the statement was believable. To encourage this reflective process, they were required to explain why they viewed a statement as 'true' or 'false'.

Each individual was required to make up his or her own mind and then the group as a whole was required to reach consensus about the veracity or 'truth value' of each idea. Reaching a measure of agreement necessitates conversations between children, critical listening and negotiation.

As a strategy for presenting a ramped demand that will gradually induct children into the procedure, educators can ensure that the ideas included for initial consideration are easy to decide upon, so readily classifiable as members of one or other of the two sets, 'true' or 'false'. When uncertainties creep into the decision-making process, as when children realise they are unable to make up their minds about some statements, a third category of 'not sure' or 'can't tell' is useful. Once the decision making is complete, the adult can probe the nature of the 'not sure' difficulty to ascertain the reasons for uncertainty. The intention of such conversations is not to correct children but to treat 'not knowing' as a legitimate state. Uncertainty can be understood as an opportunity for finding out more and used to guide children to the realisation that it is in their power to collect more information to resolve their uncertainty. This restores their sense of ownership and control over their own learning and dissipates any sense of disappointment of being 'wrong'.

These early attempts by teachers to scaffold young children's conversations so that they are enabled to critique and evaluate the truth-value of statements are essential to the later consideration of the validity of scientific arguments. Later, they will be expected to weigh the evidence to decide whether an idea (or 'claim') can be supported.

Reflection

Consider a science activity you have taught or plan to teach in which children express their ideas and you notice some:

1. ideas that you think are relevant
2. ideas that are difficult to understand
3. statements emerge that you think are irrelevant
4. ideas you consider important, which are missing.

How could you deal with each of these circumstances to further your goal of evidence-based discourse between early years children?

More subtle than decision making centred on 'true' or 'false' is the scenario in which children are invited to reflect on science claims or propositions put forward by others and to consider whether they 'agree' or 'disagree'. In these instances, they are required to critique the idea and the reasoning backing it and compare the other's view with their own. As familiarity and assurance with this quality of exchange grows, children will increasingly probe and challenge each other's ideas. Educators must make the rules for these transactions explicit: in coming to a conclusion as to whether they agree or not, they must explain their reasoning. They might offer a line of reasoning that links different ideas together, which elucidates why some ideas are discounted and others accepted. They might suggest alternative ideas and gradually demonstrate the capability to show why these improve the claim. Our observations in the course of classroom-based research with teachers persuade us that there is good reason for adults to be ambitious with respect to the standards that can be achieved in such exchanges. We have observed children in early years settings showing impressive competency to express ideas, justify their viewpoint with reasons and engage in a thoughtful critique of ideas proposed by others.

Pause for thought

Teacher guided discourse

The stimulus and starting point for a group of children's (aged 5 and 6) discussion of materials was an old painted boat in the school grounds. Children climbed in, examined the surfaces with their hands and talked about the materials used to make it. In their literacy work on speaking and listening they had gained experience and some skill in listening carefully and responding meaningfully to one another's utterances. These skills were deployed and developed further in a science context of materials. The teacher closely supported the dialogue between children.

Teacher (T):   We are going to listen very, very carefully now and think about whether we agree or disagree with each other's ideas about the materials used to make the boat, and why.

Jo: Screws are made out of metal and the green bit isn't.

T: OK. What is the green bit made out of, Jo?

Jo:	Wood, and screws are not.
Eleanor:	I think Jo's idea is true but when you paint the metal it looks like it is made out of wood.
T:	Ah! The metal looks like the wood because it is painted the same colour as the wood.
Lydia:	I know why they decided to build it from wood: because to keep it waterproof.
T:	Ah! So they decided to build the boat from wood to keep it waterproof. So, is wood a waterproof material then?

(The group responded in unison with either 'No!' or 'Yes!', suggesting they were divided in their understanding as to whether or not wood is waterproof.)

Erin:	No, because it's not a soft material.
T:	Because it is not a soft material. So are waterproof materials soft? (Note the reflecting back of the expressed idea and its reformulation as a question.)
Erin:	Yes.
T:	Has anyone else got anything to say about Erin's idea?
Anna:	I don't think that that's true because I only think waterproof materials are made out of plastic.
T:	Anyone got anything else to say about those ideas?
Lydia:	I am beginning to change my mind because actually I think plastic is waterproof.
T:	But what about wood?
Lydia:	Wood can rot in the rain so I don't think it is waterproof.
Anna:	Plastic doesn't rot down so I think Lydia's idea is true.
T:	What do you think about wood then? Do you think wood is a waterproof material?
Anna:	Wood is not, because if you leave it outside for a long time, it will rot down.

(Continued)

(Continued)

T: Has anyone got anything else that they could say linked to that?

Lewis: If you jump on the boat it will just break because it is plastic.

T: What do you think the boat is made of? (Teacher seems to be checking out the child's understanding.)

He knocks the boat to check or test his ideas: 'Out of wood'. (Tapping the boat shows the child is looking for evidence through testing as part of the conversation.)

Development of such competency depends on an educator's long-term strategy and determination to establish a regime in which all participants understand the skills and the expectations within the social ethos. The educator's role will need to be far from *laissez-faire*. For example:

a. The teacher's explicit encouragement of thinking will need to include direct requests for reasoning about each idea, both from the child expressing the idea and from other children.
b. Competencies in listening to, critiquing and responding to others' ideas may need a similarly directed request from the educator to establish the 'serious' nature of the discourse. (By 'serious' we mean not flippant, off-the-cuff or poorly considered.)

Listening to and critiquing each other's ideas so that weaknesses or strengths in an idea or the supporting evidence might be spotted are integral to constructing new understandings. For example, in 'Pause for thought: teacher guided discourse', listening to Anna's idea that plastic is waterproof caused Lydia to rethink her own understanding and begin to change her belief that wood is waterproof. She showed awareness that her ideas were changing and made the group aware of her insight. She was able to explain why her understanding was changing, describing explicitly how she had been influenced by other children's ideas. An emerging capability to think critically and to monitor changes in understanding is apparent.

There are important aspects of this teacher's practice in supporting the discussion process that helped to develop understanding of the properties of materials. She drew attention to vocabulary by asking children in an open-ended manner to suggest alternative words for 'break'. She posed probing questions to review and clarify understandings in lines of reasoning that were not clear. For instance, Lewis reveals an unexpected view that the boat is made from plastic. The teacher checked Lewis's idea and in reaction to his teacher's query, he tapped the boat, leading him to a revised conclusion that the boat is made from wood. This is an example of a formative assessment cycle that was completed in seconds. Monitoring these exchanges is demanding of the teacher who must actively listen, keep track of the flow of the argument and intervene judiciously as part of the exchange.

The science content agenda for the discussion, the properties of materials, was clearly planned and managed by the teacher. At the same time, she cued children to the fact that the intention was for them to be active in expressing and sharing their thoughts and for them to decide if they agreed or disagreed with points made. In short, her support required:

a. a clear curriculum agenda
b. planning of an engaging context and material resources
c. active awareness and support of the direction of the discussion
d. a form of 'power sharing' or distribution of ownership that consisted of encouraging children's expression and exchange of ideas, 'child-to-child' as well as 'child-to-teacher'.

The focus up to this point has been on ideas and reasoning expressed in speech with direct experiences or concrete objects providing a stimulus or starting point for ideas. Children's own drawings or 3-D models can also serve as a medium of expression and are particularly valuable when they are integrated with speech. They provide a reference point for shared, unambiguous understanding of the arguments being proposed. They can also help children to keep track of the different threads of thinking. Ideas in drawings and models can be compared and justified in similar ways to ideas represented in speech, but with the added support and advantage of a concrete referent – the object under consideration.

Pause for thought

Physical objects as reference points for discussion

A group of 5 and 6 year olds was asked to apply their knowledge of materials and sound to make their own outdoor musical instruments. Their teacher described her aims as being to develop their capabilities

(Continued)

(Continued)

to listen and respond to others, as well as the aspiration to enhance their understanding of materials. As she explained, her intention was thus to support both conceptual and procedural understanding:

> Prior to designing and making their outdoor musical instrument, the children had already built up a basic knowledge and under-standing of materials and their properties. They were able to name common materials and use words to describe them, for example, 'hard', 'soft', 'bendy' and some more advanced vocabu-lary (e.g. 'transparent'). The children had also developed their ability to listen to others' ideas and reply constructively while referring to a word bank, with encouragement and prompting. In order to further the children's understanding of how and why materials are used and also to further develop their ability to listen and reply to others, I decided to take them outside on a materials walk. I decided that the activity should take place in the rain so that the children could observe and learn from first-hand experiences about how materials react when they get wet.
>
> (Teacher of 5–6 year olds)

Children used their knowledge of the effects of rain on materials to design and make their musical instruments. Small group discussions chaired by the teacher allowed each in turn to justify their design and choice of materials and respond to each other's inputs. In the following transcript, Jack's cardboard drum forms an integral part of the children's reasoning as they draw attention to various features.

Charlie: I disagree about some materials. Because, the cardboard, if the rain landed on it, it will just get soggy.

Jack: But I am going to put sticky tape all around it. It doesn't get all wet and soggy.

Charlie: If you are going to put sticky tape on, how are you going to paint it?

Jack: I am going to paint it under. Leave the paint to dry and then put the sticky tape over it. See-through one.

The children have listened attentively and posed questions that require Jack to justify his design. They signal where they question his ideas and offer advice to improve the design. The exchange can be understood as a form of peer assessment or review in which children give and receive feedback on a piece of work. The children are familiar with the approach and during the conversation, show the confidence to respond to each other's ideas independently of the teacher. They express an idea, offer justifications, spot weaknesses, offer a contrary proposal and draw conclusions in the form of an acceptance or rejection of a proposition. This is only possible as the result of the expert guidance to which they have been exposed previously.

These skills form the basis for the development of more complex reasoned exchanges in what will become known later as scientific 'argumentation'. We have set out the process of argumentation as it is formally discussed and used to analyse exchanges between older students and professional scientists. This is not with any expectation that sophisticated and elaborated argumentation using the formal terms introduced here is remotely expected in early years education. (In fact, it might be a rarity in everyday exchanges between adults!) However, we are convinced that the germs of these processes are accessible to young children. Looking back at the transcripts reproduced above can be considered as evidence that confirms this claim.

Ideas supported with justifications are central to scientific thinking in that science understandings are drawn upon and used to link claims and ideas to evidence. Stated formally, argumentation involves children in proposing an idea or claim, offering data or information collected from their enquiries to support their claim and explaining in what manner the evidence offers support. Other children who are participating in this dialogue evaluate the claim and the evidence to support it and decide the truth-value of the claim. They may be persuaded of the truth of the claim by the strength of the evidence and may accept both the claim and the evidence used to support it. On the other hand, they may challenge or rebut the claim by pointing to weaknesses in the argument. In some arguments, a counter-claim supported with evidence might be proposed which challenges the initial claim. Children's competency in reasoning with evidence is central to their conceptual development. Although the processes in the early years may not be so formally structured as in the manner described above, it is nonetheless via these kinds of exchanges that ideas are assembled and new understandings achieved.

From the expression of ideas towards scientific argument

'Argumentation' in the context of science education does not imply hostility or argumentativeness. Argument, in the sense of reasoning with evidence, provides a rational and orderly method for justifying or determining the validity of a claim or deciding between competing claims. Angry exchanges, personal criticisms and ridicule are of no purpose when the aim is to construct considered points of view and new understandings. A claim, in this context of exchange of ideas, is shorthand for, 'This is what I think is the truth of the matter.'. The argumentation procedure also carries an expectation of a response: 'And if you believe differently, please be so kind as to tell me your idea: set out how it differs from mine, and how you justify your position.' So it is not a form of combat so much as a structured and formal way of describing how people construct their ideas, offer evidence to support their point of view and argue their case in the face of counter-claims.

Reflection

Imagine you are to discuss with parents and carers how you encourage the development of speaking and listening so that the foundations for children's later development of scientific argument are in place. How will you describe your approach and your expectations for children's development as communicators and as emergent scientists? What advice could you offer carers that might extend these objectives in support of argumentation into the home environment?

Innovative science teaching and learning has paid significant attention to scientific argumentation. 'Critique' (Sinnott-Armstrong and Fogelin, 2010) in the form of constructive criticism, is an important feature of furthering understanding. It is in the listening and critical challenge to arguments that weaknesses in evidence or reasoning might be identified and new understandings constructed. The processes involved in argumentation are therefore understood to be central to children's developing understanding of science and a critically important mode of working scientifically.

Summary

This chapter has confirmed the pleasing communication and reasoning capabilities that early years children show within the framework of an informed regime: the ability to justify their ideas with reasons and to participate in discussions in which they listen and respond to one another's ideas. We have suggested that a pedagogy that fosters development from the early expression of science ideas towards the capability to reason with evidence can be facilitated by a number of means:

- establishing a safe, positive ethos in which all expressions of ideas are valued
- encouraging children to express ideas in different modes, including speech, drawing, movement, etc.
- asking open-ended probing questions which expect thoughtful responses rather than recall
- expecting ideas to be accompanied by a reason and increasingly, a justification. This may require adults to challenge children's expressions of the kind, 'It's just what I think.'
- providing explicit opportunities for children to reflect on their own ideas and to make, for example, 'true'/'false' or 'agree'/'disagree' decisions
- expecting children to listen actively and to respond meaningfully to one another's ideas
- managing interactions around real objects to reduce ambiguity and to enhance the prospects of checking claims against the evidence
- recognising and attending to children's conceptual difficulties so that the expression and critique of ideas helps children to construct new understandings
- acknowledging and supporting instances when children's ideas have changed, and celebrating these as positive instances of learning.

7

The uses of technology to support learning

Chapter overview

This chapter describes how technology can be used as one of a number of tools to enhance children's early learning in science when integrated judiciously into developmentally appropriate early years practices. The different ways in which technology's affordances can be deployed are discussed. The intention is to show how children themselves may explore, express, share and develop their ideas and experiences when its use is aligned to learning. Although discussed within a separate chapter, we assume and recommend an approach that moves children in the direction of a seamless integration of technology into their learning.

Thoughtful use of technology

We live in the age of software applications or 'Apps' and virtual realities in which important others can be present even at a distance. Children grow up appreciating that they are able to control screens kinaesthetically using touch, taps and swipes. The limits of 'concrete operational thinking' are challenged by the fact that children know that what they control onscreen can represent both concrete and abstract versions of their personal, social and material worlds. They may interact with avatars and even enter digital worlds as players in role-play scenarios, expressing intentions, desires and emotions via a digital interface.

There is increasing evidence that when technology is integrated into the learning environment and used as part of developmentally appropriate practice in which children experiment, explore and make choices, it can help them to learn how to take turns, interact and collaborate. It can also support children in learning how to find and use information (Haughland, 1999; Heft and Swaminathan, 2002). Blanchard and Moore (2010), in a white paper on the impact of the digital world on children's emergent literacy, report on how children's use of digital toys that help them to create and record stories contribute to emergent language development. Some studies have shown that children's access to digital educational media is linked to gains in literacy and language development (Kirkorian and Pempek, 2013; Formby, 2014). Investigations in multimodal cognition compared children's interactions with direct multi-touch screens and paper-based mark making. The researchers report increased finger skill and the widening of touch repertoires amongst nursery children aged 18 months to 3 years old (Crescenzi et al., 2014), implying that touch screens seem to help children to become more dextrous.

A comparison of the impact of interactions with multi-touch screens and mouse and keyboard technologies involving 6 and 7 year olds reported increased performance in maths linked to touch screens (Segal, 2011). Devices requiring a wide range of actions, including touch and physical movement, exploit multimodal learning possibilities and encourage physical interactions thought to be similar to our natural responses to physical objects. These physical interactions need not require direct touch. Designers are increasingly attending to how gestures which are integral to everyday communication, such as hand waving, head nodding, toe tapping, finger pointing, etc., can be incorporated into interactions with digital devices to support learning. The accumulating evidence suggests that performance is improved where the physical movements involved in some digital interactions resonate with and support the internal mental operations. For instance, tapping with a finger on a screen to count cubes resonates with discrete counting actions. This action contrasts with a sliding finger motion that may be more useful for quantifying a continuous substance – such as filling up a glass with liquid. Segal (2011) acknowledges that interactions should be meaningful for learning and emphasises that gestures that map onto learned concepts offer benefits to young children because they support the construction of improved mental representations. The potential of innovations in the design of interfaces and in pedagogy for the enhancement of learning is widely recognised and is the focus of work by a number of researchers (see, for example, the Embodied Design Research Group at University of California Berkeley, K-16).

Following a meta-review of technology-related research, Higgins et al. (2012) remind practitioners and policy makers that the challenge is to ensure technology is used purposefully, to enable teaching and learning practices or to make them more efficient. We are mindful of some of the apprehensions surrounding the use of technologies. Amongst these have been concerns about possible effects of over exposure on brain development, behaviour, sleep patterns, social skills, emotional well-being, academic development and language (Common Sense Media, 2011). The UK National Institute for Health and Care Excellence (NICE, 2015) advises TV-free days and a limit of two hours per day of screen time to ensure children maintain a healthy weight. Similarly, the American Academy of Pediatrics (AAP, 2011) recommends limiting screen time to 1–2 hours per day for children above two years and discourages screen access for the under twos, though with the exception of using screens to maintain contact with family members. Children's interactions with different screens will inevitably vary, leading to claims that, while the amount of time they spend may be important, the context and content of that exposure and children's individual needs may also be important (Tandon et al., 2011). There is an awareness that some recreational screen experiences with no defined endpoint are deliberately created to absorb the user and are thus difficult to put down. Issues surrounding child protection in the context of technology are also well-recognised. These include ensuring the avoidance of access to inappropriate content, inappropriate communications between users and the need to safeguard the safety of young children. What follows in this chapter is a focus on the imaginative and creative use of technology to support developmentally appropriate teaching and learning in science. It is assumed that the reader is aware of and will have strategies in place to assure the monitoring and effective response to matters of children's safety and well-being.

When to use digital technology

Decisions about when technology should be used might be guided by the following considerations.

Firstly, digital technologies might be selected when their use is expected to help children achieve outcomes that would not otherwise be possible. When blended with direct modes of early years activities and used within interactive approaches, technology has the potential to create new opportunities to engage children's minds and personalise and extend their learning. The needs of children should be uppermost in educators' minds, with technology being selected (by children or by adults) on the grounds that it helps children to reach particular goals that might not have been attained without it. Using technology should not be thought of as an end itself.

Secondly, improving access to learning resources is an important reason for drawing on technology. For instance, technology offers the potential to provide children with up-to-date resources, as in the form of interactive 3-D and virtual or augmented reality games, that enable children to access environments that would otherwise be beyond the direct reach of early years provision. Information about planets in space, life under the sea or living things in the distant past all become accessible to children through animations and immersive reality where users can make gestures in space to control onscreen objects. These offer more than passive observation and enable children to interact with environments from perspectives that are impossible to make available in real life. The development of text to voice and voice to text software is a flourishing area that can improve access. Innovations around gesture and haptics (tactile sensations linked to digital applications) offer creative and intuitive opportunities to all children, including those with additional needs.

Availability of technology in the home

Technology is in widespread use in the home and children are familiar with it in various forms from birth. Many children bring from home to their early years settings their own experience of technology and associated expectations of personal access to a source of interest, pleasure and learning. Access to a range of media begins early and is wide ranging. These media invite new possibilities for the ways in which children learn, including the potential for joint actions, social collective learning and discussion around devices. Inter-generational learning with extended family members is also opened up as a possibility.

Pause for thought

Early experience

Even with extremely limited access, at 15 months Charlotte has learned – possibly through observation and trial-and-error – to hold the device appropriately and move her fingers across the screen to turn pages. Already, she uses her toy phone to mimic conversations with others.

(Continued)

(Continued)

As well as learning some social behaviours in relation to using the digital device, she has learned that she can control the device and effect changes in the pictures and sounds it makes. Her developing attitude and approach to learning that is being established during these early interactions will enhance her confidence as she encounters other electronic devices.

Figure 7.1   Awareness of electronic devices may be gained early

Surveys in the US report that over half the children in the 0–8 years age range have access to mobile devices such as smart phones and tablets and two-thirds of families with children have internet and computer access (Common Sense Media, 2011). Ofcom (2014), in their UK study of *Children and Parents' Media Use and Attitudes*, report that two-thirds (65%) of 3–4 year olds have home access to tablet computers and 80% have access to computers, PCs or netbooks. Personal ownership of tablets amongst 3–4 year olds was at 11%. Similar patterns of home access were reported for 5–7 year olds. Two-thirds (65%) of 5–7 year olds have access to tablet computers and four-fifths (84%) have home access to computers or netbooks. Almost a quarter (23%) of 5–7 year olds owned their own tablet.

In contrast to home access, a UK survey of early years settings (3–5 years) reveals that two-fifths of practitioners reported children having access to touch screen technologies (Formby, 2014). McPake et al. (2013) have explored 3 and 4 year olds' interactions with digital toys and games in the home over several years. They draw attention to the need for practitioners to build on children's familial experiences with digital technologies and develop communicative skills in imaginative and creative ways as they enter formal schooling. In the UK, there are examples of schools within which children have devices that are used both at home and school. Systematic arrangements are in place for devices purchased through school to be used at home, or for children to use their own technology in school (an initiative referred to as 'bring your own device/technology' or BYOD/BYOT). These initiatives extend access and open up new possibilities for crossing boundaries between learning at home and school. Use of technology means that children's learning is not bounded by the formal hours of schooling and the many contexts for informal learning of science at home can be shared and built upon at school. Parents and carers explain that the shared use of technology has given them a window onto their children's learning and development. As one parent explained:

> When different animals and insects were brought into school for children to see and handle, my son took a video on his tablet. I could actually see the animals that he had seen as if I were there with him. We could talk about it with both of us really sharing the experience.
>
> (Parent of a 6 year old child)

Devices that children may wear such as glasses, watches and T-shirts having in-built digital technology are available or in the public's awareness. These have the potential to extend the possibilities for technology-supported learning.

The integration of technology into early years education undoubtedly requires careful evaluation for selective, safe and creative use in developmentally appropriate ways to support, excite and enthuse learners.

Reflection

How do you see technology being used in your establishment (or a setting or school with which you are familiar)? How do you think technology might be used to support learning and development in science in ways that might not be possible otherwise?

Encouraging the use of digital technologies in science

Technology offers opportunities for children to discover new ways of locating information. It also extends the ways in which they might represent information and their ideas. Initially, digital interactions can be expected to be exploratory, complementing the physical direct experiences traditionally offered. Very young children might engage in exploration and experiment with digital tools in playful ways such as through role-play and make-believe, augmented with digital toys and tools such as supermarket and library scanners, cameras, voice recorders, computers, printers, tablets or phones. These early experiences support and extend play and active learning by offering new roles and scenarios and possibly shifts in power and control favouring children. Capturing events using cameras or voice recorders means that a record of an episode can be shared, reflected upon and reinterpreted. Revisiting an event recorded digitally enables children to discuss the episode, make new observations and connections and build upon earlier ideas.

Pause for thought

Extending imaginative play using digital cameras

Plastic dinosaurs are commonly part of young children's play. In their recreational acting out, children tend to explore features such as teeth and claws, speculate on where dinosaurs lived and how they became extinct.

One pair of 4 and 5 year olds chose to take a photograph of their dinosaurs – an idea that was quickly adopted by others. With the teacher's help, the children printed their images. One example included the incorporation of a prop to show a dinosaur eating a biscuit (see Figure 7.2). This creative, open-ended activity was part of a playful exploration of the dinosaurs. Children being paired encouraged collaborative play, helped to ensure they took turns, discussed ideas, listened to each other and agreed decisions. The children's use of the camera, encouraged by the teacher, gave them ownership and control. As well as ensuring they had a permanent record of this experience, the photographs provided a concrete product that might stimulate further discussions between children: 'What did dinosaurs eat? Were there any people around to feed them biscuits? How big were they?' Their teacher elaborated on how the pictures led to some high-quality creative writing about the 'naughty dinosaurs' and that the humorous photographs improved children's engagement, collaborative working and learning outcomes.

Figure 7.2 Creating imaginary contexts for dinosaurs

Using technology to find information

With teacher support and increased exposure to a range of digital tools, children might be expected to move from exploration and play activities to investigate and find information to help answer some of their own questions. Some of these enquiries may be in relation to questions raised by children that seek new knowledge such as, 'What is …?' (conceptual knowledge) and others might be of the kind that ask, 'How do I do this?' (procedural knowledge). Learning how to locate factual information and how to find out about procedures for doing things are both related to the emergence of working scientifically. Enquiries supported by digital technologies can be blended with searches for information in books, video, etc. and by consulting experts to enrich and enhance the information collected through any single technique.

Information gathering enquiries might involve children in searches of material that their teacher has made available on an organisation's intranet or on closed websites to which the children have been provided with secure access. Technology offers enhanced access to new content and a richer information resource in the sense that the modes in which information is presented are extended to include video, images and audio as well as text. Children can be empowered to make their own searches using their own search terms. Placing carefully judged limits on the volume of material made available will ensure that they will not be overwhelmed and will be more likely to have a successful and fruitful experience.

Pause for thought

Using technology to find information

The group of 4 and 5 year old children shown in Figure 7.3 is exploring the idea of animal extinction. They are using a computer attached to the interactive whiteboard (IWB) to search for animals they think are extinct. The information they are reviewing has been placed by their teacher on a closed sharing website which the children have permission to access. There is a little competition initially for control of the mouse but the individuals soon agree to take turns. As they move through the website, different animals appear simultaneously on the computer screen and on the IWB. Using both screens helps children to share and discuss their ideas. They point animatedly at the images of animals as they talk, identifying parts of the organisms worthy of closer attention. They discuss each animal as it appears and decide whether it might be extinct. Those they agree to be of interest are selected and placed in a folder on the desktop. The activity is open-ended, engages their attention and facilitates critical review of the information collected, all involving social interaction. Technology has enabled them to search for information and to locate and select animals that may not otherwise have been available to them. Furthermore, the mode of operating has encouraged collaboration, discussion, reflection and the social skill of taking turns, as well as oracy skills. The learning outcomes for the children are enhanced knowledge and understanding of the world, and incidentally, increased awareness of the uses of technology in gathering and storing information.

Figure 7.3   Finding, sharing and discussing information

Devices for enhancing observations

Binoculars and telescopes are useful for seeing objects at a distance more clearly, but as with hand lenses, children have to be supported if they are to use them effectively. Getting observed objects into focus is a skill that has to be acquired and younger children may become impatient with the fact that instant success is unlikely. Digital magnification is another way of transforming available information to observe selected features more closely. High power enlargement is not needed and may actually interfere with children's capability to interpret images as they lose the link between the real object and the image. Up to 10x magnification is ample, and children can be helped to develop the habit of making drawn notes of what they can see. Digital visualisers or microscopes can be linked to IWBs and used by individuals, or to greater advantage, with groups or the whole class. The group context is an excellent platform for nurturing collective thinking and the negotiation of both the vocabulary to name and the interpretation of the function of what is observed. Handheld probes with modest magnification attached to a computer help improve children's observations of, for example, potato shoots, the structure of pieces of material, frogspawn and tadpoles, etc.

Pause for thought

Digital magnification

Children 3–5 years of age use small handheld probes connected by USB to the computer to improve their observations of frogspawn. Children carefully hold the probe over the bowl of frogspawn; the magnified images can be viewed onscreen, enabling the observation of features that would not otherwise be observable. 'It's moving'. 'That one has a white spot in the middle'. 'Are they brown?' 'Look, that one has a tail'. The children are fascinated by their observations. Initial competition to use the device subsides after a while. Eventually, children learn to use the device independently of an adult, but they may initially need adult help and encouragement to hold the probe steady so that the object being observed is clear and in focus.

Figure 7.4 Using technology to take a closer look at tadpoles

Temperature, sound and light sensors can be used to enhance observations and help children make discriminations that may not be possible using the human senses alone. For example, as part of children's exploration of habitats, light and temperature at the trunk of a tree might be compared with an open area of the school field. Sensors may also help to introduce children to a variety of means of representing data. Working between children's own representations of charts and tables and the representations generated by sensing devices attached to computers can be helpful in supporting developing understanding. Six and seven year olds using light sensors to find out, for example, 'Which materials let most light through?', were asked by their teacher, 'If you weren't doing your graph on the computer, how would you draw it on the paper? How would you set up your graph?'. To show the class her idea, one of the children gestured with an index finger at arm's length (a superb example of acting out understanding using body movement, incidentally) to show the shape of the x and y axes. 'You would draw like an L and on the bottom bit of the L you would write the different pieces of materials and down there you would write how much light'. Children were just getting to grips with making charts and graphs and the technology offered them welcome support in displaying their results as charts, graphs, tables, etc. The educator encouraged children to reflect on the graph shown on the computer and to think critically and actively about the steps involved in producing their own chart or graph on paper. In addition to enhancing children's observations, the teacher realised in the technology novel and timely opportunities to bring together and discuss developing understanding of maths and science recording skills. The drawings with an arm in the air, on paper and via a computer screen are complementary multimodal representations, different ways of communicating understanding of the relationship between axes on a chart or graph.

Using cameras to enhance and record observations

Cameras or camera functionality in devices such as tablets, provide the possibility of children capturing images at a distance that may otherwise be difficult to view close up. They might then use the image magnification function to observe the colour and markings or shapes of specific features. Time-lapse photography or video might also be used to capture events that happen imperceptibly over a long period of time such as the germination of a seed, the opening of a flower or the emergence of a butterfly from its pupal stage. Static camera images can be viewed sequentially while video allows replay to show changes speeded up, enabling children to view the entire process in a brief period. Such technologies help to form bridges between children's outdoor and indoor learning and between learning at home and in settings. A photograph allows an event that has captured a child's interest (possibly at a different time or place) to be shared with others, discussed and possibly reinterpreted. Learning thus continues across the traditional boundaries of time and place. Photographs might be printed off and presented in large floor books or wall displays or shared and celebrated via large digital screens and tablets. Participating in and contributing to these events allows children to work collaboratively, discuss details, ask questions of one another and engage in dialogue about an event that has been recorded very simply and easily. Increasingly, children may decide for themselves, guided by their own interest and goals, when to use still or video cameras to record an event that interests them.

Pause for thought

Using digital cameras to record observations

The 3 year old in Figure 7.5 uses her camera to capture a photo of the fish at the aquarium she is visiting with her nursery. She notices the brightly coloured fish and some of its different features and takes a photograph. She later refers to the photograph to help her describe to her peers and to her parents some of the specimens that caught her attention. While some of the features could be seen directly, the photographs allow her to consider at leisure the relative size, the different shapes, colours and patterns and some of the features that she might have overlooked in real time. Capturing images provides children with valuable personal resources that help them to record, remember and describe the detail of what might be unique opportunities to observe marine animals, etc. up close.

Figure 7.5   Recording images of fish for later discussion

Using technology to support the expression of ideas

There is a well-established, respected and legitimate early years emphasis on the development of language skills. A major theme running throughout this book is the importance of encouraging all children, whatever their unique needs, to access and make known their ideas in as many different modes as is possible. Multimedia technologies offer children a resource that can be used to extend their expressive repertoire. They increasingly exploit video, audio, images, colour, 3-D models as well as speech, text, touch, whole body physical actions and gesturing in space to offer children these affordances for the expression of ideas. Rather than (as sometimes expressed as an apprehension) undermining language use, expressing ideas in different modes enriches and extends children's capabilities to share understandings.

Assembling information from a number of sources

An increasing range of software applications is available that is dedicated to helping with the combination of multimedia resources with text. These technologies allow sharing of products within the group or across classes and more widely. For example, digital applications designed with young children in mind help them to create stories, digital comic strips, animations, video and posters using their own digital images. Children might use simple audio tools to provide a commentary for their photographs. User-friendly microphones can be attached to computers via a USB to make voice recordings. Where children have drawn pictures, these can be scanned and incorporated into e-books and comic strips. Online video authoring sites designed for young children, along with increased availability of smartphones and tablets that have the capability to capture moving and still images and sound, enable children to create video and audio sequences and cartoons straightforwardly. For instance, 6 and 7 year olds exploring growing foodstuff and cooking food agreed questions they wanted to ask of the school cook. They recorded their interviews with the cook on smartphones and tablets. In other contexts, photos of plants at different stages of growth and pieces of melting ice children had observed were inserted into a video application together with a voiceover to create a video story. Text, speech, drawings, images, sounds, music and special effects can all be incorporated to help children express their ideas in a much richer manner than has ever been possible previously.

Pause for thought

Collecting digital information from different sources

A visit to a zoo provided the starting point for one 6 year old's personal research into some of the animals she observed. The meerkat was her favourite animal and although meerkats proved to be too elusive to observe details, taking a photograph enabled her to capture and zoom into the image, making the shapes of the paws visible. Using the software in her tablet, she was able to add sound recordings to the accumulating images as she moved around the zoo. During the visit, children referred to the information collected on each other's devices as they discussed the features, sounds and behaviours of the animals they had seen.

Tigers are species that are very dangerous and they eat chicken and roe meat. Lions are also like tigers they eat the same things.

What do tigers eat?

What other animal are like tigers?

Are tigers dangerous?

Do they like chickens?

Are they the same pattern as lions?

People think elephants are not dangerous but they are! They can stamp on you and if you are not careful they can run after you in Africa. African elephants have bigger ears than Indian elephants these elephants are Indian.

- What are the animals called on the piece of paper?
- Are they a lot of elephants in the wild?
- Do you like elephants?

Figure 7.6 A digitally created hardcopy book made by a child

On her return to school, she continued her personal enquiries, finding further information in books and the internet. Combining the different sources of information, she made a hard copy book that she was able to share with other children. The software she elected to use enabled her to add text and her own images to assemble her ideas about the different animals. She selected her page layout, font, image size and position in relation to the text. The pictures were used to convey the visual information; text permitted adding ideas about the animals' behaviour and people's views about them. She combined the information learned about the animals with questions to encourage other children to think about her ideas and to reflect on their own reactions and feelings. The digital tools helped this child to produce a product that she was proud to share.

Using technology to access distant scenarios

DVDs, CDs, software applications and 3-D augmented and immersive reality technologies extend children's access to information beyond their immediate environment. Distant scenarios and otherwise inaccessible environments are made available to them to explore in 3-D. Immersing children in these contexts may provide them with carefully sequenced challenges which, in a game environment, might result in gaining points, moving up levels and earning badges as they learn. These tools engage and empower children and reinforce learning. Children are enabled to inform themselves actively, negotiate unfamiliar environments safely, take risks and manipulate the milieu in ways which tend not be possible in real-life contexts.

Webcams can be used to help children gather information by watching events in real time that would otherwise be unavailable to them, perhaps because they happen outdoors and are difficult to access or happen outside the school day. Webcams can provide valuable 24/7 insights into animals' behaviours that would not otherwise be directly accessible, such as that of nesting birds, hatching caterpillar eggs, nocturnal animals, etc.

Pause for thought

Webcam enabling 24-hour access

A school's webcam provided children with 24-hour access to incubating hens' eggs. Children were able to continue to observe the hatching of the incubating chicks from home, outside school hours, by accessing the school intranet. The technology enabled children to observe the shells cracking and the chicks emerging. Some 4 and 5 year olds (with parents' help) captured screen grabs of the chicks to share with classmates the following day. (The children were also able to observe an adult's hand stroking the chicks

(Continued)

(Continued)

when they thought school was empty! The event sparked children's curiosity and interest and prompted a parallel enquiry aimed at tracking down the identity of the adult using the evidence of the features of the hand caught onscreen.) Using technologies in these creative and imaginative ways encouraged collaborative interactions between children and between children and their parents that centred on school events. Additionally, they extend children's experience and knowledge of science by providing access to events that might otherwise have been missed.

Figure 7.7 Observing changes at a distance that would otherwise be missed

Real time recordable video 'feeds' can also be used for data collection and for testing ideas (hypotheses), as when nest-box cameras are used to monitor feeding frequency, time taken to fledge, and so on.

Reflection

Imagine a 'show and tell' session in your class or group. How different from traditional performances would it be if children used technology to support their presentations? What impacts do you think various forms of technology might have on children's listening skills, interactions between children, the quality of the ideas expressed and the feedback offered?

Using technology to find out about procedures

To locate procedural or 'how to' information, children can access immediate and detailed help using video sharing sites and age-appropriate social media. Faced with challenges such as 'How can I make ice lollies?', or 'How do I make bubble mixture?', these sites are increasingly becoming one of their ports of call. Video sites provide multimedia guidance about how particular processes might be carried out, often posted by experts who are very likely to turn out to be peers rather than adults. Additionally, they provide environments (with safety assured) for children to share and celebrate their own developing skills. These experiences of peers as experts may in turn modify the children's developing understanding of 'expert' and 'expertise'.

Communicating with others at a distance

Digital tools extend the possibilities of discourse or more informal conversations between individuals and communities beyond the family, class and school. For those just coming to terms with their developing capability to express ideas and having those ideas listened to, opportunities to interact with people nationally and internationally need to be seen as exciting possibilities rather than daunting prospects. The early years age group always seems to exceed expectations in handling technology. The assurance of children's safety in any interaction, whether face-to-face or online, will need to be of paramount concern. The prospect of conversations beyond the school presents particular issues with which teachers need to be familiar. In the first instance, parents need to be informed and kept up-to-date about the uses of any technology in school. According to an Ofcom (2014) report on the use of technology by children aged 3–4 and 5–15 years, most parents mediate children's use of technology. Only a small minority (5%) of parents did not mediate their children's use of technology in any way. A culture needs to be established which recognises, monitors and supports children's growing digital competencies and the changing vulnerabilities associated with them. Evidence and research in relation to safeguarding children in the context of digital technologies can be found in Byron (2010) and United Kingdom Council for Child Internet Safety (UKSSIS, 2015). Guidance and training for educators and parents can be found for example, at the Child Exploitation and Online Protection Centre (CEOP, 2015) and the National Society for Protection of Cruelty to Children (NSPCC, 2015).

A school's closed intranet provides the possibility of children communicating with each other and their teachers within school hours and this can be extended from school to home. Children might have individual pass-word-protected access to video, quizzes, activities, blogs and other resources placed on the intranet by their staff or by class members. In some schools, children communicate with their peers in different groups or classes over the internet. Using software packages or online functionality, it is possible for children to express ideas in voice, text or images and for these to be shared and responded to in real time by children in another class within the same school. For example, children collecting information from their school's weather station were helped to broadcast their results across the school. These tools add another dimension to communications and make it possible to pool, compare or critique results with a wider group of children beyond the class.

Some children may be familiar with home use of texts and emails. Very young children with family members in different parts of the world are particularly likely to be familiar with widely available free video conferencing facilities or Voice Over the Internet Protocol (VOIP), software that permits video and voice exchanges nationally and internationally. These tools allow family members to interact regularly with a young infant at a time of rapid change and development. By the time children reach 4 years, they may be sufficiently acquainted with communicating in this way that they may initiate these calls themselves, under supervision. The availability of free video conferencing has meant the wider use of this software by children and adults. Some parents of early years children permit them to use these technologies to continue their conversations with friends outside the school day. Schools might make use of children's increasing familiarity with emails and video conferencing in their communications with partner schools across the world. Issues likely to be of common interest are not difficult to identify: people, hobbies, pets, animals, food, playgrounds, weather and environment are some examples of the content areas that young children might discuss during these exchanges. Such interactions, supported by their teachers, help young children to access and weigh up alternative views and experiences.

A 'blog' or 'web log' is a kind of diary or regular update of news and views using the World Wide Web. An individual child, group or class can publish a secure blog that allows ideas, photographs and text to be broadcast in an informal style. For example, one class of 6 and 7 year olds invited their families to visit their class museum. The museum displayed children's collections. Models, photographs, drawings and writings about dinosaurs, fossils and rocks were displayed with carefully prepared labels. Pictures from the museum open day were published on the class's secure blog. Blogs offer the possibility of exchange of feedback with an audience within and beyond the school around issues of personal interest to children. Those having some science relevance might include caring for the family or school animals and sharing details of their growth, development and behaviour. Children's (successful and unsuccessful) attempts to grow various plants, or to create a vegetable garden might be shared. School visits might feature, as might enthusiasms for collections of various kinds. Used safely and securely, blogs have the potential to encourage social collaborative learning in which expertise is exchanged and developed.

To engage fruitfully in these peer-to-peer interactions, children should be aware of 'netiquette': how to give and receive feedback positively without causing offence. Incidentally, explicit training for and rehearsal of how to conduct thoughtful online exchanges is extremely relevant to learning how to conduct themselves in face-to-face argumentation procedures.

Digital technologies used in developmentally appropriate and creative ways encourage collaborative and individual learning. Responsive guidance and oversight from adults will ensure that children remain focused on the learning goals, build on their ideas and achieve successful outcomes.

Summary

Using digital technologies in developmentally appropriate ways offers various affordances to early years learning.

- Technology-supported learning extends the modes through which children can access, share and develop their understandings. It offers all children a multimedia resource that can be used creatively and imaginatively to extend their expressive repertoire. The availability of video, audio, still images, colour, 3-D models as well as speech, text and touch broadens the understandings that can be accessed and expressed using any single mode alone or in combination.
- This chapter has shown how digital technologies can be used in open-ended ways to offer communicative and creative possibilities for collaborative and personal enquiries that engage and motivate and contribute to both collective and personal understanding.

(Continued)

(Continued)

Encouraging children's capability to select and use digital tools appropriately to support and enhance their learning is a positive contribution towards the development of independent, resilient and empowered learners.

- Technology supported learning enhances the scope of science observations and extends the quality and range of access to evidence that children might use. It offers access to observations, real or virtual, that are not available to human senses alone, including the possibility of exploring distant, dangerous or inaccessible environments and events that interest children.
- Children are invited and encouraged by technology's enhanced communicative possibilities to think creatively, reason and make decisions about the relevance and reliability of new information that they have accessed and how it might be recorded and presented for a range of audiences. Used alongside a range of practices to support collaborative interactions at home and at school, and to encourage and extend the feedback possibilities, technology can be a productive feature of teaching and learning any time, any place.

Planning, assessment and record keeping

Principles of planning, assessment and record keeping for science

The responsibility for planning learning experiences in science, evaluating outcomes and keeping track of children's progress via efficient record keeping procedures resides with the managing adults, and in turn, the organisation that employs them. The benefits of these evaluative activities accrue to a wider set of stakeholders: parents, carers and especially the children themselves. Occasionally, other professionals will request information about children's progress and well-being. We suggest that, rather than think of these processes as purely an adult obligation (and one sometimes regarded as an onerous but necessary chore, almost like taking the fun away), a broader perspective that integrates them into a wider-ranging view of pedagogy makes more sense. In his review of assessment, Black (2015) acknowledges the view that many teachers see assessment as a peripheral part of pedagogy. By integrating planning, assessment and recording within the broader values that attract people to working with young children, educators' work experience will be more satisfying as well as more productive. These responsibilities need to be reconciled with the broader aim of promoting the science development of children who have minds and special science interests of their own; can think for themselves; express their interests; have their own views of the activities in which they would wish to spend their time and energy; are capable of reaching their own conclusions about whether or not they are satisfied with their enquiries and whether or not they would like to modify the way they do things next time around. Encouraging the participation of children in the evaluation of their learning and focusing feedback on task-specific criteria early in their development helps children appreciate that learning is something that can be developed and improved, something that they can change; their achievements understood as something they themselves can influence. Their attribution of success to factors they can control, such as 'effort' rather than to 'luck' is detailed in a line of research spanning two decades (Dweck, 2000). Consulting with children in relation to their achievements and next steps helps them to develop the skills to respond actively and positively to feedback to improve their learning outcomes.

Our overall stance is 'child sensitive' rather than 'child-centred' because it takes the view that the adult must retain charge of the broader science agenda and oversee children's progress. This includes signalling clearly the framework of acceptable values and behaviour within which children's personal choices can be made. It is an outlook that requires a careful devolving and sharing of responsibilities (and the privileges that go with them) between adult and child, in a spirit of mutual respect. It acknowledges that children can and should be consulted and involved in planning and evaluating their own science enthusiasms. Science is special in the sense that the entire world and beyond offers an infinite range of legitimate opportunities and interests that children might choose to pursue.

Formative assessment or 'assessment for learning' is a process that should be taking place in the course of teachers' everyday science interactions with children. Evidence from classrooms gathered by the authors over many years leads us to a formulation that describes recurring cycles of interaction between children and educators. The skills required of educators for the adoption of formative assessment techniques are described in a detailed sequence in the following pages, set out in a manner that makes clear how the approach can be incorporated readily into early years daily science practice. Each phase is exemplified. Dialogue with children is of central importance so that, as with planning, their education is something children are consciously involved in thinking about, rather than something done to them.

Approaches to planning and assessment that involve children lead naturally to a similar perspective on record keeping: children can and should be involved and be aware that their successes and their progress are recognised and celebrated, with their positive achievements foregrounded. The volume and quality of data capture available to education has expanded enormously in recent times and this changes the relationship between formative and summative assessment. Children have opportunities to select, document and retain digitally their own most valued achievements, for example through personal portfolios. The role of the adult is to initiate the lifelong processes through which a self-regulating dialogue is established inside children's heads: 'How am I doing? How would I like to improve? What is the way forward for me?', and so forth. This self-monitoring must avoid taking the form of perfectionism where the learning ethos is one in which errors are pounced upon. A supportive and rational environment peopled by 'critical friends' (people who are well-disposed, positive and constructive in their guidance but do not shrink from honest advice) can be established by the initiation of techniques of peer- and self-assessment. In this manner, a sense of failure that might cause embarrassment can be avoided and risks and challenges are more likely to elicit coping strategies rather than avoidance due to apprehension about possible mistakes.

Pause for thought

Peer feedback

A group of 4 year olds was observing the daffodils they had planted outside. Their teacher recalled for them that they had planted the bulbs some weeks back and advised them, 'Remember, I'm looking for a picture to tell the story of what has happened to the bulbs'. The children's actions and comments confirmed that they understood the context and their teacher's request for accurate drawings. One boy moved between

(Continued)

(Continued)

the actual flowers and his drawing table, gesturing to the petals and explaining, 'I've drawn those in yellow'. The teacher invited the group to turn over their drawings so that they could focus on each individual's drawing in turn. As children contributed, she repeated their idea responsively to help ensure that all had heard the comment and to show that feedback was valued. One of the children, Chloe, explained her drawing, 'The rain comes down and the Sun is there. The water makes the flowers come up'. The teacher turned to another child, Lexie, who was keen to offer her view of where the Sun should have been drawn. Lexie commented, 'The Sun should be up there, in the sky'. 'Why did you think that?' asked the teacher. Lexie responded, 'The Sun makes it warm in the sky'. Another child added, 'So the flowers grow'. The children's comments confirmed they were listening, responsive to the feedback and adding their own relevant ideas. The teacher asked the group if they had all heard Lexie's idea. She placed an arm around Chloe and asked, 'When your friends have looked at your picture and you were listening to them, did you like what they said? Do you want to change your picture now?'. The teacher's verbal and non-verbal behaviour, particularly towards the child receiving feedback, provided a safe and reassuring milieu in which the children could reflect on their work and give and receive feedback with confidence. She carefully and deliberately checked out how the child handled the peer comments, recognising the emotional, social and cognitive dimensions of peer feedback.

Planning for what?

Plans are what all people of whatever age, in whatever occupation, use to anticipate and rehearse future actions and events. People organise so as to be prepared for what might happen, whenever it might happen and however unexpected the form it takes. What do we need to prepare for in early years science education? We can divide concerns into firstly, the paramount obligation of being prepared to look after the health and well-being of children and secondly, preparation for meeting their curricular needs. Preparations must take account of routine, expected events as well as the unexpected.

It is in the nature of much science education to be exploratory and to take activities from the mundane into less familiar areas. Digging in the soil, handling plants and animals, cooking and eating various ingredients, perhaps visiting a farm or handling and observing different materials: all of these entail possible risks but can be enjoyed perfectly securely with basic health and safety built into planning. Appropriate preparation can liberate rather than constrain activities. Science educators take safety very seriously and helpful advice is available in publications such as that from the Association for Science Education (ASE, 2007) and on similar organisations' websites. Health and safety planning needs to be built into practice, with provision also for emergency action: procedures, contact numbers and first aid equipment.

Pause for thought

Risk assessment

Good relationships with parents are important. Keeping them informed about activities is vital, particularly so when children are likely to come into close contact with animals. It is essential to check parental permissions and whether any children have particular requirements, e.g. they may only be able to touch animals while wearing gloves, etc. Ensure parents know that hygiene and risk assessment procedures are in place for any activity requiring them. Children should be informed that they must not put their fingers in their mouths or noses and ensure they wash their hands well after observing animals.

Introducing children to animals and plants offers significant opportunities for establishing caring attitudes, just as the way young children handle soft toys is used in the early years as a model for taking care of one another. Children take the lead from adults, so it is important that sensitivity towards all living things be demonstrated, and this should include 'minibeasts', or small invertebrates (animals without backbones, or 'without vertebrae').

Background science

Classification of living things

The way all living things are ordered is called 'taxonomy'. There are seven levels: kingdom, phylum, class, order, family, genus, and species. There are five kingdoms (though the single-celled monera and protista kingdoms may be sub-divided). More familiar are the fungi, plant and animal kingdoms. The scientific name of every known species uses the

(Continued)

(Continued)

two-part (binomial) system invented by the Swedish biologist, Carl Linneaeus. The first word, the genus, is capitalised; the second word is the species. Both the words are written in Latin italics. We modern humans are therefore *Homo sapiens*. Until about 30,000 years ago we shared the genus with *Homo neanderthalensis*, now extinct, but interbreeding is confirmed by genetic evidence.

Phobias centred on invertebrates are occasionally encountered, but mild or more entrenched negative attitudes are more common even amongst adults. Every effort must be made to avoid transferring such mind-sets to children. Even referring to creatures as 'creepy-crawlies' communicates negativity, just as does the mindless annihilation of any uninvited organism found in domestic space. Children like to handle small creatures but would be better simply observing and being taught to do so with extreme care, always returning creatures to their habitat. Likewise, plants should be left in place. The fate of the slipper orchid, plucked to extinction, is salutary.

Outdoor areas, both immediately adjacent to school rooms and further afield, offer rich resources for science planning, irrespective of weather conditions. The adage, 'There's no such thing as unsuitable weather: only unsuitable clothing', is expressive of the attitudes of outdoor education advocates, such as the international Forest School movement (www.forest schools.com/a-history). There are expectations as to how these open access outdoor areas should be used, most countries having their own 'countryside code'. These refer to respecting other users and the local community, leaving gates and property as found, following paths, leaving no trace of the visit, taking litter home and following the advice on signs. Where fire is a particular hazard, precautionary advice needs to be followed.

Reflection

How could you extend your planning by increasing the possibilities of your outdoor practice in imaginative ways? What are the gains for children in being outdoors that would not be available indoors? What safety and other issues need to be considered compared with indoor activities?

Planning for science curriculum coverage

'How am I going to keep all those active, energetic minds interested and occupied in something to do with science during next week? Next month? For the whole year?'. 'How do we go about planning some science for young children?'. The answer is to be rational, curious and excited about possibilities and especially to remember that science is all-pervasive. There are certain touchstones to refer to, questions to ask that will offer ways forward:

- Children's own needs and enthusiasms: what are young children interested in and what do they like to get involved with?
- Staff pastimes and expertise: what special interests, hobbies and enthusiasms do you and other staff have that could be shared with children?
- School context: are there special issues related to the local context, geography, economic circumstances, industry or demographics that are worthy of particular attention?
- Forthcoming events: what opportunities are on the horizon, perhaps locally, nationally or internationally, in the calendar, such as festivals or events in the news?
- Statutory or regulatory curriculum requirements: how may any or all of the above be adapted to be consistent with requirements expressed in the curriculum to which your organisation refers?

Itemising the local and personal considerations before more formal curricular obligations (as above) reflects the suggested priorities. This scanning for suitable contexts is a deliberately 'bottom up' strategy. Starting from the reality of the local situation and allowing children's unique interests to grow and find expression through more formally worded goals means that the energy that drives children's enthusiasms can be harnessed. Orientation and motivation will have been established already.

We encourage an approach to science in the early years from a holistic and cross-curricular perspective, accepting that the priorities for young children must be acknowledged as the establishment of positive relationships, communication and language skills, ensuring healthy physical development and safeguarding personal welfare, social and emotional development. But science issues do not need to be regarded as stand-alone or 'bolted on' extras to broader curricular targets. Science can be treated as complementary or even integral to wider curricular frameworks and areas of learning and development that shape activities in early years settings. In this way, children's science interests can be seamlessly integrated with other areas of the curriculum, within enabling environments that respond to children's individual needs as opportunities arise.

Planning for science content coverage

By 'content' is meant the subject matter identified with science. Science content can be accessed through everyday contexts and in the early years such an approach is to be favoured. While there is no reason to exclude specifically science contexts such as opportunities to discuss the work of scientists, their laboratories and special apparatus, for young children, the emphasis can be on science as including thinking and reasoning, having curiosity about the everyday world. The subject matter about which to foster interest and curiosity can include themselves and other people and virtually every encounter in the world that can be observed, classified, named and reflected upon. Everything is novel, so of interest, or capable of being made interesting – even that which is mundane to the adult viewpoint. Take time as an example: how time passes and how we record its passing. Think about the passage of day and night, sunrise and sunset, how the light changes and the way we describe it. And then there are the seasons, with the opportunities each offers: growth and reproduction in Spring; bright Sun, short deep shadows and lush growth of leaves and flowers in Summer; cooling weather, shorter days and falling leaves in Autumn; cold winds, ice and snow, freezing water, icicles melting, how we keep our homes and our bodies warm in Winter.

Background science

The seasons

If we think of a line going through the Earth from North Pole to South Pole, that line (like a skewer through an orange) is not perfectly vertical to the Sun. The consequence is that the rays of light energy from the Sun do not always pass through the Earth's atmosphere by the shortest route, which would be at right angles. The effect of going through the Earth's atmosphere at a different angle is a longer journey for the light, so we feel less of the Sun's heat. At such times, we also see the Sun as appearing to be lower in the sky – unlike at the equator, where the Sun appears to be directly overhead at midday. The other important factor in causing us to experience seasons is that the 'skewer' wobbles over the course of a year, altering the angle at which the Sun's rays reach our part of the Earth. When the Sun's rays reach us more directly, we experience higher temperatures and more hours of daylight. This is our summer in the Northern half (hemisphere) of the Earth. The change in the angle of the tilt means that at that same time, people in the Southern Hemisphere will be experiencing Winter. So the idea often expressed by children, that of the Earth moving closer to the Sun being the cause of Summer, has no basis in science.

All these everyday contexts are rich in possibilities when coupled with and driven by children's individual interests and curiosity. For adults, there might be a need to see the familiar with fresh eyes (actually, a renewed attitude of mind) by being enquiring and asking questions.

Preparation is essential, but beware over-preparation to the extent that there is no time to be enthused by and dwell upon unexpected events. In a science context, everything is interesting, including disruption: storms, floods, falling trees, broken windows, leaking roofs, animals or plants being in the wrong place or at the wrong time. 'Why has this happened?' is a good starting point and an opportunity not to be missed. If the subject of interest is falling leaves and it turns out that insects start crawling out onto tables, make use of the event and celebrate the uninvited guests by observing, recording, discussing and finding out more. These crossover possibilities can work both ways. If the planned focus of children creating stories stimulated by a walk in the woods is children's speaking and listening skills and it turns out children become interested in some of the plants and animals around them, this interest can be built upon. Children's unanticipated enthusiasms and curiosity about their local environment can be drawn upon to engage them in science as well as creative expression activities. With experience, as particular themes or contexts are revisited, greater flexibility will become incorporated into planning and confidence will grow. This greater self-assurance will help to avoid shutting off possibilities of reactive planning, when unexpected but potentially enabling opportunities that arise can be exploited.

Another important consideration in every planned science activity is to think of three phases: planning and preparing materials and resources prior to the event; managing children's engagement during the activity; and the aftermath – clearing up, of course (and children can learn their role in 'housekeeping' activities), but more importantly, reflection on what the children gained from the experience. All three phases are important, but it is perhaps the third that may be most easily neglected when time presses. This is unfortunate as it is children's (and teachers') transformation or re-representation of the experience after the event that we emphasise as critical to successful learning.

Assessment

There must be integration of: (i) planning for science curriculum coverage; (ii) the delivery of the curriculum through teaching and learning experiences; and (iii) assessment and record keeping. This section discusses assessment but assumes a coherent overview in which these different processes complement one another. Achieving this harmonious blend requires careful reflection and preparation. Integration emerges with experience of repeat cycles of activity from which lessons are learned and glitches ironed out. To work in an educational and developmental context requires us to understand the subtleties of procedures and purposes of assessment. For sure, there will be times when any and every educator will be drawn into the debate, both with colleagues and parents, as to whether assessment is a 'friend' or 'foe' (Black, 1997). The principles need to be rehearsed and understood, for they are at the heart of professional practice.

The fact is that assessment is an integral part of life, from beginning to end. In the developed world and wherever resources allow, every baby ever born is given a head-to-toe physical examination immediately (or within 48 hours) of entering the world. Skin tone, posture, symmetry, sounds of the heart and lungs, infant reflexes (the Moro clinging reflex, sucking and hand grasp) are all checked. Assessment and examinations are a pervasive and essential aspect of life. So diagnostic examinations happen at both extremes of life, and 'exams' (as we come to know them) punctuate all points in between.

Assessment, tests and examinations

The most important way of classifying any and all forms of assessment that draws on the observation and measurement of children's science performance is from the perspective of its *purpose*, the use to which the results are put. There are three main uses:

- **Formative** – that seeks to find out where a learner is in their development and understanding, so that the experiences provided (educational interventions) may be tailored to a particular child's requirements.
- **Summative** – an assessment that 'sums up' performance by drawing a line under it, albeit perhaps a temporary mark that may be used to inform a decision justifying one action in preference to the alternatives. For example, a choice of the next step to be taken in educational provision may be needed. The summative performance data can be pointed to as the evidence at one point in time, used to inform a judgement about the future.
- **Diagnostic** – that has clinical connotations in seeking to analyse something that appears to be going not as expected, perhaps in speech, hearing, reading, writing, number, or science understanding, for example. Diagnostic data is used to inform decisions about putting things right, or remedial action.

There is considerable overlap between these three purposes. They all depend on observing (or sometimes, measuring) some aspect of the learner's performance – not necessarily all of the relevant behaviour, but more likely a sample. Furthermore, the sample must be representative. Many teachers practice continuous assessment, recording and annotating examples of pupils' science work with their own formative or diagnostic comments over time.

The children's work is the teacher's evidence base and informs their teaching interventions. It allows teachers to distinguish different qualities of performance and shape children's experiences accordingly to meet individual needs. Only when a summing up is required, such as when a child completes a phase, or moves class, or school, or a report to parents is required is the very same detailed formative evidence base distilled into much briefer summative conclusions. The data accumulated continuously during day-to-day interactions over time and across a range of contexts that has enabled the teacher to respond to individual needs and monitor progress towards goals are capable of being used to describe individual children's different capabilities or achievements for summative purposes. These summative judgements reveal where children have reached the expected goals, and where they have exceeded or have not yet reached them. Should any point in a summative statement be of particular interest or contested, the report in question should be capable of being traced back to the evidence against which it is justified. There should be congruence between the criteria against which summative judgements are formed and those informing the daily formative decisions that ensure the tailoring of experiences to children's unique needs. The 'not yet' summative statements might be thought of as having formative potential since the term implies a position along a dynamic continuum towards a learning target that has not yet been reached. An agenda for formative action for the child and the teacher is thus implied in the term 'not yet reached'.

Pause for thought

Recording options

A teacher with responsibility for the care of 4 and 5 year olds noted children's ideas as one of a number of approaches she used regularly to help keep track of children's developing science skills, and consequently, respond to individual needs.

> As part of my practice I use a variety of methods for recording speaking activities. These include written observations, voice recordings and mini-pictures. I record speaking activities regularly in order to monitor and assess the children's progress and to keep evidence of their skill acquisition in science. I can then use this information to inform future planning.
>
> (Teacher of 4–5 year olds.)
>
> *(Continued)*

(Continued)

Typically, she would record each child's idea together with the children's names and arrange them on a wall chart together with photographs. Approaches that include using floor books or wall displays that children can access as and when they choose extend the period of reflection and consolidation. Children develop confidence as they come to realise that their own ideas are interesting to others and confirm the imaginative range on offer, including examples of capabilities to which they might aspire.

The greater the volume of evidence against which an assessment judgement is based, the more reliable it tends to become. As digital storage of large volumes of examples of children's work becomes easier to capture, manage, search and retrieve (including images, scans, perhaps video and audio of science enquiries that might have been conducted by groups of children), the evidence base that can be accrued for each individual has grown enormously. There are both advantages and dangers inherent in digital storage. Increasingly, software applications have become available to educators that enable the recording of children's achievements against curriculum requirements in real time using tablets and other mobile devices. The great advantage is that the distinction between formative and summative data and its uses fades; the same up-to-date collection of evidence to inform current teaching for formative purposes can be surveyed and summarised for summative purposes, as and when required. For example, perhaps a child moves location or develops some kind of problem needing expert intervention. The accumulated data can be précised for summative purposes into a summary version. But here's the danger: a mass of information will be overwhelming if it is not organised and structured very carefully at the time it is collected and stored. Unorganised collected snippets do not constitute data collection. This is better characterised as deferred record keeping. Careful planning and organisation will avoid frustration and stress when the need arises to comb through a backlog of random evidence to make sense of it. And of course, records in whatever form need to be backed up as their loss can be catastrophic.

Reflection

How do you store your records of children's achievements? If you handed them over to a colleague, could they make sense of them and find their way around? If you had the time, how would your perfect system of record keeping look? What is the best practical compromise you can arrive at?

A formative assessment cycle

In its general principles, assessing science is mostly no different to assessing any other area of the curriculum, but there are some aspects that will be given particular attention. In the early years, formative assessment must ideally be

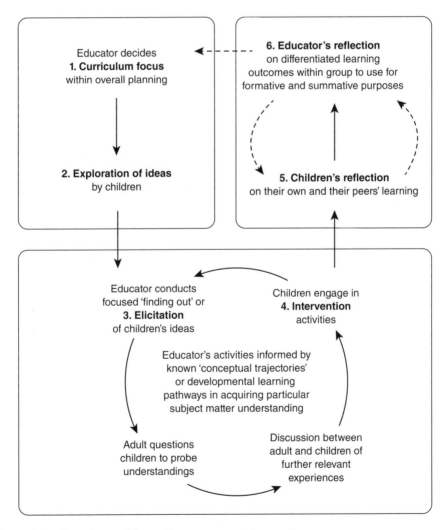

Figure 8.1 Flowchart of formative assessment in practice

fully integrated into everyday practice, complemented by efficient record keeping and guided by planning. Figure 8.1 summarises a formative assessment cycle. For clarity, each step will be discussed in detail, bearing in mind the proficient practitioner will be able to move flexibly and adaptably between children at different points in the cycle. The procedure will sometimes consist of very brief cycles of just a few seconds with an individual child. At other times, the cycle may involve a few weeks' work with a whole group. It is designed as a checklist, a kind of touchstone to review progress and should not be allowed to become a bureaucratic formula to be followed slavishly.

The previous chapters have frequently discussed and presented contexts and referred to using formative assessment. Here, the processes involved are examined in detail. The phases are described as general principles initially, before moving to some fleshed out examples.

1. *The (science) curriculum focus* indicates the learning agenda set by the educator's planning. While we assume a 'child-sensitive' approach in which each learner's current capability is the starting point, there should be no doubt that adults need to be orchestrating the learning environment with clear objectives in mind. (Occasional precocious science performances by children can be cherished, but they need adults' management of a stimulating learning environment to enable them to happen.)
2. *Exploration of ideas* is a phase during which children 'catch on' to the context, subject matter, expectations and opportunities within the experience the adult has planned. Direct experiences are particularly helpful in clearing ambiguities about what the teacher has in mind. The opportunity for children to orientate their thinking by handling materials and objects is an excellent way of angling children towards the educator's agenda.
3. *Elicitation* or 'finding out ideas' is where children are deliberately encouraged by the learning environments provided to express their thoughts: verbally, in actions or drawings or any of the modes discussed earlier.
4. *Intervention* implies that the adult influences what is happening in some manner, however invisible this may be to the children concerned and no matter how avowedly child-centred the adult's practice. Children can be enticed into an activity by their own curiosity, attracted by the fact of certain materials being available and catching their eye and imagination. Adult mediation includes the continuous day-to-day identification of different qualities of understanding during interactions with children and the tailoring of interventions in direct response to children's needs and expressed understandings to facilitate progress.
5. *Children's reflection* refers to children growing in confidence as resilient learners, thinking about their own ideas and contributing positively to the learning of other children. This phase can be too easily overlooked,

resulting in activity without contemplation. The 'hands-on' interactive technology centres use a constructive slogan, 'Hands on, brains on', that sums up what is needed. Children's experiences gain from extension from action to re-representation in thought, language and other modes. Also, the fact of children recognising that others may have ideas that differ from their own is one early step towards appreciating the need for offering justification for their own ideas.

6. *Educator's reflection* includes listening and responding to children's ideas along with an overall view of the effectiveness of the activities that have just been made available. Additionally, there may be a summing up of achievements against the early learning goals or performance outcomes. In England, this may occur as children are approaching the transition between EYFS and KS1 or between KS1 and KS2. The model accommo- dates summative judgements informed by the rich detail in the accumulated continuous data of children's achievements. A useful formative outcome would be to identify minor or major adjustments to improve the experi- ence and learning outcomes in the future. Duschl and Gitomer (1997) suggest that teachers' assessment of *cognitive* goals in science (that is, the quality of any learning that might, or might not, have occurred) tends to be overlooked or subsumed in favour of *activity* goals (the routines used during the management of science enquiry) in the classroom. They also point to the difficulty some educators feel in allowing children to take own- ership of the learning activity. This difficulty in relinquishing control might be due to a particular sense of what it is to be a teacher; that is, the person who takes responsibility for all the details of what happens in science activities, rather than encouraging possible serendipity and imaginative innovations in children's responses. An educator's preparedness to modify learning objectives 'on the hoof' in response to children's interests and when special circumstances arise is likely to develop with experience.

Assessment cycle: some illustrations of practice

We can now trace several possible journeys through the process so as to illustrate the formative assessment cycle in science in a more concrete manner. The context used throughout is that of plant growth and more specifically, the germination and growth of seeds. No single line of enquiry is anticipated, as we have to bear in mind the range of children of different ages, interests and capabilities and the variety of possible interesting offshoots they are likely to pursue. The 3–7 age range encompasses an enormous diversity of capability, needs and interests and we can expect the adults managing the experiences to encourage the topic to develop in an assortment of ways.

The common factor is the sequence of procedures, plus the fact that, in all cases, children will be exploring and finding out about their world. In this illustration, the focus is on learning about some aspects of the plants that inhabit it. Bear in mind also that the brief cameos used to illustrate the steps through the process serve to confirm the continuity in the flow of events as we move through the cycle. A greater range of other possibilities for each phase with more detail is detailed in earlier chapters, so it might be found profitable to refer back occasionally to some of those instances.

Phase 1: curriculum focus

It is for the adults to decide the curriculum focus, but the context of germination and growing from seeds has much to commend it as an example. Precedent confirms that children always find it to be a fascinating hands-on topic. Spring and summer might be the best time for this topic, as seeds would be likely to germinate readily without propagators or other special equipment. There are seeds that germinate well in the autumn and even winter sowing is not impossible. Children's activities could include thinking about what plants and seeds are, where they are to be found, observation of different forms of seed, how deep to plant, anticipating the time for germination and conditions required for growth. Some children might be expected to take their explorations further, comparing the growth of plants and recording their results. The teachers might be seeking to increase children's awareness of growth from seeds through observation, discussion, comparison, measurement and recording. Children might also learn about the variation in living things that they were likely otherwise to treat as identical. Teachers' planning could include setting the scene with relevant stories, images and artefacts. Preparation of resources would be needed, either outdoors if ground is available, or using compost and seed trays indoors, under cloches or in a greenhouse or sunny window sill. If conditions for growth were to be the subject of enquiry, the quality or measured comparisons in different locations might be explored.

Phase 2: exploration of ideas

Educators must provide experiences that will warm children to the topic, to avoid hitting them unawares. Presenting the activity as a set of directives with seeds and instructions would take ownership away from the children, so that they might wonder why they are doing things. Images of plants and flowers germinating, growing and being cared for could be put on walls and discussed with children when they notice them. Relevant story and reference books could be placed where they are going to be encountered. Suitable stories could be researched, to be read to children as an introduction to the topic (for example, *Ten Seeds* by Ruth Brown, 2010). Children could be provided with many different sizes, shapes and colours of seeds (as shown in Figure 8.2) to observe and discuss. Interesting questions might be rehearsed in preparation for discussion sessions: 'Has anyone grown seeds at home?'; 'What plants do we grow from seed?'; 'What is the biggest seed in the world?'; 'Do all plants have seeds?'; 'Do we eat seeds?'; 'What do you think seeds need to grow?'; 'Do all the seeds in a packet grow exactly the same?'; 'What would we see inside a seed if we looked through a microscope?'. These questions are used to trigger the discussions that set the scene for the next phase, when teachers will encourage the expression of ideas between children and engage them in further discussion. This allows adults to gain an appreciation of children's current thinking.

Figure 8.2 A variety of seeds to examine

Phase 3: elicitation

At this point, the adult's intention will be to ascertain children's pre-existing beliefs and interests about seeds, their germination and growth, perhaps conditions for growth, depending on the agenda set. Plans for moving into some form of exploration or enquiry may need to be modified from the original intention, and associated learning objectives adjusted in response to children's interests or the unexpected ideas expressed. Ideas can be invited from the whole group, perhaps interrupting a story to tempt the voicing of points of view. Children could be paired to prepare their viewpoint jointly, or a slightly more formal procedure using individual written or drawn expressions of ideas could be used. It is worthwhile noting or getting children to record their initial ideas because once they begin their learning they will rapidly forget their former ideas. They may even deny that they ever believed such things, not through embarrassment, but simply because they now hold different ideas.

Phase 4: intervention

In the context in which we use it to discuss teaching and learning about science, 'intervention' is not used in the sense of direction by an adult. We think of it as interactions that bring about a transformation of some kind from the original situation or understanding so that there is a conceptual change. That change might involve simply observing over time something that had never been witnessed previously. This could result in a pattern or difference being observed, talked about and recorded that tells the child something new compared with what had been known initially. For example, children might observe the process of germination of a seed that is kept moist and warm but visible rather than buried in soil (Figure 8.3). This is a wondrous and seemingly magical event for children to watch and perhaps draw or photograph over several days. (They might also be invited to draw what they think happens inside the seed before and during germination – a drawing of their belief rather than their perception.)

Figure 8.3 The magic of seeds beginning to germinate

A range of possibilities is available for intervention in the form of explorations and enquiries as shown in Figures 8.4 and 8.5: observing, comparing the growth of different seeds and in some instances eating the

Figure 8.4   Long-term planning: raised beds

Figure 8.5   Long-term planning: waterproof labels

edible parts; practical investigations in the form of 'fair tests'; research using secondary sources such as books, the internet and multimedia resources; and experimenting with the cut and thrust of reasoned, evidence-based discussion with peers.

Phase 5: children's reflection

Children become very much involved with the doing of enquiries, which is very satisfying for them and their educators. To gain maximum value from their enquiries, they would need to expend at least as much time and determination thinking about, discussing, interpreting and explaining the results of their work. In some sense, every episode in which a child is asked to reflect on and express what they believe is also an intervention. Every act of conscious reflection helps to crystallise thinking by encouraging what was inchoate to become articulated. We are asking these young minds to verbalise their thoughts and this is challenging for them. That act of representation changes their understanding by refining and elaborating what they are aware of knowing. It is important to capitalise on this opportunity to consolidate from experience to knowledge.

It becomes very much easier for children to reflect on the outcomes of their enquiries when they are able to compare like with like, with just one factor (or 'variable') changed at a time. This is not always possible and there is always something to be gained from discussing outcomes. For example, the experience of growing carrots outdoors in the soil is very different from that of growing sunflowers indoors in pots of compost. Commercial compost is likely to be sterile, meaning that no self-sown wild seeds will germinate. Children may be puzzled by several differently shaped leaves appearing in their seed bed. Unexpected events like this should not be treated as an unwanted intrusion or contamination. The emergence of 'weeds' (that is, any plant growing where not invited) can be treated as interesting rather than a troublesome intrusion on our planning. 'Where have these other seedlings come from? Did someone plant them? Have they also grown from seeds? Which are the carrots we planted? How can we find out?' Anything that stimulates more questions and further enquiry is of great interest from the point of view of learning the questioning attitude that is characteristic of science.

A comparison within or between enquiries is much easier when quantification of some kind is used, as shown in Figures 8.6 and 8.7. For example, the heights that seedlings have grown can be compared: either directly, side-by-side; using non-standard measures (finger widths, perhaps); or standard measures, cm and mm.

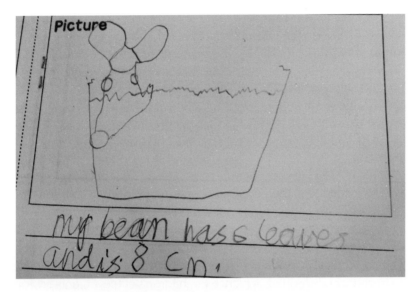

Figure 8.6 Bean diary record

Figure 8.7 Quantifying observation by counting leaves

Phase 6: teacher reflection

The assessment cycle will have provided evidence to record within children's individual learning 'histories' or 'journeys' whether in digital or hard copy format. It will also have told teachers and indeed children a great deal about several important aspects of the topic:

- the range of ideas and interests that prevail amongst the group
- the understanding, capabilities, needs and interests of individuals
- the kinds of gains in understanding that are possible through the use of particular interventions
- useful resources to make available when the topic is revisited, perhaps next year (raised beds or garden area to be developed; use of laminated waterproof labels; recycled materials for plant pots; collecting seeds for next season, etc.).

The detailed evidence gathered continuously in relation to children's achievements and needs provides a rich multimodal resource that can be used to inform the summative assessment process either at the end of the year or at transition points. When required, the recorded achievements of each child should be capable of contributing to the summative assessments. Our perspective is to treat the collection of evidence of children's achievements for formative and summative purposes as closely linked, essentially the same information but used for different purposes. The accumulation of wisdom can be translated into revised plans for revisiting the topic, perhaps the following year.

Formative assessment is something done *with* children rather than *to* them. Involving them in the process is essential to negotiating personal learning targets, to reviewing where they are in relation to those targets and what they have to do in order to progress towards the desired outcome and to developing them as successful, confident and resilient learners. Formative assessment must invite answers to the question, 'What teaching-learning experience comes next?'.

Reflection

Think through an activity that you have undertaken with children or that you are planning to undertake. Draft two or three sentences against each of the six phases for that activity. Which phases tend to be overlooked under the pressures of daily practice? What are the consequences? Can you think of a way of changing things so that the entire cycle is taken into account?

Milestones, norms and criteria

It is instructive to unpack the figures of speech used to label children's educational progress in science. This will help to clarify the underlying meanings and this in turn might serve to make the debate around them more rational, less fevered. Throughout this book, we have referred to children's developmental progression in their learning of the various aspects of science with the developmental criteria illustrated throughout. Now we turn to the concepts used to describe that progress and compare children, set targets, and so on.

A very common way of discussing child development is to speak of the passage of time as if we are thinking about distances along a route or journey. We speak of 'milestones' of development to refer to significant events. Originally, milestones were engraved stone markers set along a road to indicate the distance for stagecoaches to or from two points in a recurrent journey – clearly pre-satellite navigation. Coaches would cover a 'stage' manageable for a set of horses; we also speak of 'stages' in development. Apart from the difference of dealing with distance rather than time, physical milestones are set at fixed and measured distances in a way that is simply not the case with developmental milestones in children's science learning. For example, developmental milestones such as walking and talking or losing the first set of teeth are neither exact nor fixed points. Milestones must be understood as having an amount of chronological latitude and would be better expressed as a range. It would also be more accurate to describe these events as 'markers' or better still, 'criteria' (singular 'criterion'). A criterion is a defined reference point that allows comparisons between individuals or groups to be made. Useful criteria work if they are unambiguously binary: two-way, measures met or not met, present or absent. Useful criteria do not bend. Our advice when evaluating children's progress in science is to refer to the qualitative criteria that have been set out in earlier chapters. This would be to use 'criterion-referenced' assessment to observe and record children's science behaviours.

When discussions about children's functioning enters areas of uncertainty as to what is appropriate to expect, we often resort to consideration of what average performance would look like. The 'average' number in a series (for example, age in months of 100 toddlers when they utter their first two word sentence) is calculated by adding all the ages together and dividing by the number of children (100). The average is also referred to as the 'mean'. These simple statistics can be used to review the outcomes of criterion-referenced assessment. For example, we might review a group of children to calculate the percentage that are able to express their own ideas; the proportion having a clear concept of 'alive', or able to give a reason for their ideas.

Targets and benchmarks

The term 'benchmark', like 'milestone', is another archaic term imported for educational use. It has an interesting etymology, the original use of the term being very much concrete in nature, referring to the mark cut in a wall or pillar by a surveyor as a fixed point of elevation. On a building site, benchmarks would be used as the reference points so that when building a bridge from both sides of a river or excavating a canal, for example, all other measures would need to refer to that benchmark. Canal water would not then be expected to flow uphill and the spans of the bridge would meet in the middle. Benchmarks are extremely useful points of agreement. Going back further in the history of the term, the bench referred to the seat taken by a judge in court, the criterion being that, as representative of the crown, all other persons in the court should (and would necessarily because of his superior elevation) look up to the judge on his bench. The most important point to bear in mind about today's usage in the context of science assessment is that a benchmark does not denote a superior level of performance, as in the judge's seating position. Nowadays, the term denotes an agreed point of reference that allows things to be compared against a common standard. Benchmarks tend to be imposed from above by politicians and administrators, so it is very important that the meaning behind the requirement (the criterion) should be absolutely clear to all users.

Just like a benchmark, a 'target' is an agreed standard using a clear criterion that is commonly understood and agreed. What the word 'target' adds to the discussion is the fact that, in an educational context, it tends to be an aspiration, something to reach for rather than a performance that is already achieved. A 'clear criterion' means that the description of performance is unambiguous. 'Agreed' might be more contentious in the sense that the targets that carry force tend to be set by administrators rather than teachers and practitioners. For educators, the important consideration is whether or not the targets for science performance are realistic. Teachers and practitioners should have a view, and should certainly be consulted, as to how realistic such target setting is. For this reason if no other, an understanding of the principles outlined above is a professional necessity.

Reflection

Do you feel that your planning, assessment and record keeping practices are well-integrated? Are there practical changes you would like to make?

Summary

This chapter has explored how planned approaches to assessment in the early years are able to contribute to the development of thoughtful, independent and resilient learners.

- An underpinning principle is that formative assessment needs to be conducted continuously by educators in order that they find out the different qualities of children's performances during their interactions and respond appropriately to different needs.
- A key premise is that the collection of evidence of children's achievements for formative and summative assessment is inextricably linked. Our perspective is that the two processes proceed in tandem.
- Children benefit from being involved in the processes of assessment, record keeping and planning their own continuing learning. When carefully managed, peer assessment can also play a constructive role.
- The different purposes of formative, summative and diagnostic assessment are described. Technology now permits large volumes of information to be collected and stored, but this needs to be systematically organised to be useful. As and when required, formative data can be selectively sampled into representative summary form and used for summative purposes.
- The chapter describes a model of formative assessment derived from practice. The various phases of activity within the cycle are described with practical examples. Such sequences between educators and children can sometimes be completed in very short periods – perhaps a few seconds – as well as over longer periods of time.
- Planning, assessment and record keeping are best treated positively as an integral aspect of the educator's professional role. Because of the importance attached to assessment at the individual, institutional and national levels, educators are advised to engage with the basic assumptions and technical terms used to describe and evaluate children's developmental progress in science.

Appendix

Science subject matter for 3–7 and its assessment

This book has throughout focused on pedagogy, with suggestions about how to approach science teaching and learning of 'emergent' science. Educators of younger children tend to have concerns about what subject matter these children should be learning about and how to assess relative success across a group of children. Throughout this book there are many illustrations that refer to the subject matter of science, the concepts with which children might engage. These possibilities for teaching and learning around particular content are listed and cross-referenced by chapter below in the expectation that they may prove useful in stimulating further activity. However, we appreciate that it is likely that some readers will ask, 'What quality of understanding should I regard as acceptable?', or 'How can I decide whether children have "met", "exceeded" or "not yet reached" expectations for their performance?'. What we cannot (and do not intend to) offer in response to such queries is a set of test questions and performance benchmarks. The danger of following that route is of narrowing curriculum experiences to conform to what can be tested.

The breadth invited by the relative lack of specificity in the science content for children aged 3–7 years offers a freedom that should be grasped wholeheartedly. The means for educators to carry out their own assessments as an integral part of practice have been described in earlier chapters of this book. Such practice will enable educators to build up for themselves and their organisations a practical, evidence-based view of the different qualities of understanding of which children are capable as well as of developmental progressions or 'trajectories' in that understanding. So what we offer here is not a set of tests and performance outcomes, but something far more useful. We describe the steps in a formative assessment process that can be used continuously to build up your awareness of the different qualities of understanding that children reveal so that you can respond to their needs and support their progression. It is a process that can be used recurrently in all the contexts and referring to all the content summarised below. In fact, the process is a summary of what has been described throughout the book, in succinct form.

The steps (as part of habitual daily practice, using a formative pedagogy) proceed like this:

- Actively listen and take note of the range and quality of science-specific understanding expressed by children as they engage with your provision. This will enable you to build a picture of 'differentiation', meaning the span of different qualities of understanding across the group, both successes and confusions
- Use your growing awareness of different qualities of understanding to fine-tune tailored support
- Where possible, discuss with colleagues to compare outcomes, checking how representative your group is of performance more generally (in effect, an informal 'moderating' process)
- Try to identify some of the key foundational understandings along the typical pathway (or 'conceptual trajectory') towards the big science ideas so that you can respond flexibly and effectively to children's needs
- Use those descriptions drawn from the range of differentiated performance to describe individual children's current position in the range and needs for formative purposes (feeding back to children, reporting ongoing progress to parents, etc.)
- When required (e.g. at transition), use that same range or scale of differentiated performance to describe individual children's achievements for summative purposes against external requirements.

We strongly advocate treating formative and summative assessment in tandem, as drawing on the same underlying information about a child's performance. Whatever the science subject matter decided upon for teaching and learning, this general method for determining needs, next steps and outcomes can be applied.

Science activities and subject matter referred to in this book

Science context and subject matter content	Chapter	Page
Animals: observing frogs outdoors	1	20
Animals: using a fictional story to explore adaptation and change	2	34–5
Animals: visiting a farm	3	49
Animals: encouraging whole body movements to explore the lifecycle of a frog	4	72
Animals: using a 'road map' to tell story of dinosaurs dying out	4	74
Animals: observational drawings of aphids collected from fallen leaves	4	78
Animals: using different sources of evidence to draw animals	4	79–80
Animals: making 3-D models to show features of animals	4	81
Animals: sketching ideas about the changes going on inside an incubating egg	4	82
Animals: sketching how an animal might have changed into a fossil	4	83
Animals: observing incubating a hen's eggs	5	99
Animals: observing tadpoles, butterflies and stick insects changing	5	99
Animals: observing and talking about hens	6	115
Animals: creating imaginative environments for dinosaurs	7	136–7
Animals: finding information about animals using computers	7	138–9
Animals: using probes to help children observe frogspawn and tadpoles	7	140
Animals: visiting an aquarium	7	142
Animals: observing a butterfly emerging from a pupa	7	145
Animals: visiting a zoo	7	144
Animals: observing incubating eggs at home and at school	7	145–6
Humans: role-play involving 'doctors and patients' to explore health and parts of the body	4	73
Humans: finding out about similarities and differences between themselves and others	5	99
Plants: germinating seeds	3	56
Plants: walking through leaves and expressing ideas about them	4	69
Plants: using drama and actions to consider how tree seeds germinate and grow	4	73
Plants: making a 'memory stick' to show plant parts collected during a walk	4	75
Plants: sketching ideas about what is happening inside a seed	4	82
Plants: finding out how far away the seeds fall from the tree	5	86–8
Plants: exploring growing seeds	5	98
Plants: investigating and comparing plant growth	5	101
Plants: investigating growing tomatoes	5	103
Plants: exploring ideas about fruits and vegetables	6	120
Plants: observing the opening of a flower	7	141
Plants: exploring conditions for growing bulbs	8	153–4
Plants: observing and comparing seeds	8	166
Plants: observing germinating seeds	8	167–8

Science context and subject matter content	Chapter	Page
Plants: investigating and comparing growing plants	8	171
Living things: observing plants and animals	8	156
Living things: exploring life cycles and predator–prey relationships through narrative fiction	2	33
Living things and their habitats: observing living things in the woods	3	5
Living things: picture strip drawings of ideas about how fossils may be formed	3	56
Living things and their habitats: making models to explore what snails need to live	3	59
Living things: asking questions, handling, observing and identifying living things	4	66–7
Living things: drawing and discussing ideas about 'What's alive'	4	68
Living things and their habitats: combining evidence and ideas to make a group drawing of where and how moles live	4	79–81
Living things and their habitats: investigating the light and shade in different habitats	7	141
Materials: exploring colour mixing and painting	2	29
Materials: using a fictional story to explore properties of materials	2	31
Materials: exploring how to make water travel through pipes	3	49
Materials: handling clay to observe changes	3	50
Materials: outdoor kitchen to explore properties and changes in natural materials	3	51–3
Materials: exploring ice outdoors	3	53–5
Materials: picture strip drawings predicting changes to ice	3	56
Materials: drawing washing drying on a line	3	56
Materials: making sounds and exploring sound travelling through materials	3	57
Materials: handling, discussing and classifying sand and stones	4	67
Materials: exploring changes by squashing, stretching, pouring and sieving	4	71
Materials: cooking as a reversible change	4	73
Materials: role-play involving 'builders' to explore materials	4	73
Materials: sketching ideas about what happens to the water left in a cup	4	82
Materials: making bubbles	5	96
Materials: observing and extinguishing a candle flame	5	99
Materials: dissolving a sugar cube	5	99
Materials: exploring a melting ice cube	5	99
Materials: exploring dissolving jelly	5	99
Materials: observing and exploring evaporating puddles	5	99
Materials: observing and recording a bonfire burning	5	99
Materials: observing and recording changes in wet clothes drying	5	99
Materials: exploring which materials let light through	7	141
Materials: interviewing the school cook	7	143
Materials: exploring and discussing how materials are used	6	122–5
Environment: expressing ideas about cars	1	9
Forces: using a fictional story to investigate how to move and lift objects	2	32

(Continued)

(Continued)

References

Adey, P. (2008) *Let's Think! Handbook. A Guide to Cognitive Acceleration in the Primary School.* London: GL Assessment Ltd.

Alexander, R.J. (2008) *Towards Dialogic Teaching: Rethinking Classroom Talk* (4th edn). Dialogos.

Alexander, J.M., Johnson, K.E. and Kelley, K. (2012) 'Longitudinal analysis of the relations between opportunities to learn about science and the development of interests related to science', *Science Education,* 96: 763–86.

Allen, M. (2014) *Misconceptions in Primary Science* (2nd edn). McGraw Hill Education.

American Academy of Pediatrics (AAP) (2011) 'Policy statement – media use by children younger than 2 years', *Pediatrics,* 128(5): 1–7.

American Association for the Advancement of Science (AAAS) (2001) *Atlas of Science Literacy, Volume 1.* Washington, DC: AAAS and National Science Teachers' Association, Project 2061.

American Association for the Advancement of Science (AAAS) (2007) *Atlas of Science Literacy, Volume 2.* Washington, DC: AAAS and National Science Teachers' Association, Project 2061.

Association for Science Education (ASE) (2007) *Be Safe!* www.ase.org.uk/resources/health-and-safety-resources/health-and-safety-primary-science.

Avraamidou, L. and Osborne, J. (2009) 'The role of narrative in communicating science', *International Journal of Science Education,* 31(12): 1683–1707.

Baron-Cohen, S. (1997) *Mindblindness: Essay on Autism and the Theory of Mind.* Cambridge, MA: MIT Press.

Barsalou, L.W. (2008) 'Grounded cognition', *Annual Review of Psychology,* 59: 1–21.

Black, P.J. (1997) *Testing: Friend or Foe? Theory and Practice of Assessment and Testing* (Master Classes in Education series). London: Routledge.

Black, P. (2015) 'Formative assessment – an optimistic but incomplete vision', *Assessment in Education: Principles, Policy and Practice,* 22(1): 161–77.

Black, P. and Wiliam, D. (1998a) 'Assessment and classroom learning', *Assessment in Education,* 5(1): 7–74.

Black, P. and Wiliam, D. (1998b) 'Inside the black box: raising standards through classroom assessment', *Phi Delta Kappan,* 80(2): 139–48.

Black, P.J., Harlen, W., Russell, T., Austin, R., Bell, D., Hughes, A., Longden, K., Meadows, J., McGuigan, L., Osborne, J., Wadsworth, P. and Watt, D. (1993) and (1995) *Nuffield Primary Science SPACE Project.* Harper Collins.

Blanchard, J. and Moore, T. (2010) 'The Digital World of Young Children: Impact on Emergent Literacy. A White Paper'. Arizona State University College of Teacher Education and Leadership. Research presented by the Pearson Foundation, 1 March.

Blanquet, E. and Picholle, E. (2012) 'Inquiry based analysis of early years children's books: developing skills for later science education', in C. Bruguière, A. Tiberghien and P. Clément (eds), *E-Book Proceedings of the ESERA 2011 Conference: Science Learning and Citizenship: Part 14* (co-eds C. Constantinou and J. Johnston). Lyon, France: European Science Education Research Association, pp. 6–11.

Brown, R. (2010) *Ten Seeds.* London: Andersen Press.

Bruguière, C. and Triquet, E. (2014) 'Analysis of problem-oriented reading using the picture book *La Promesse*: learning opportunities about metamorphosis for 6- to 7-year-old children', in C.P. Constantinou, N. Papadouris and A. Hadjigeorgiou (eds), *E-Book Proceedings of the ESERA 2013 Conference: Science Education Research For Evidence-based Teaching and Coherence in Learning: Part 16* (co-eds P. Kariotoglou and T. Russell). Nicosia, Cyprus: European Science Education Research Association, pp. 3021–30.

Bruner, J. (1986) *Actual Minds, Possible Worlds.* Cambridge MA: Harvard University Press.

Byers, A.B. and Walker, C. (1995) 'Refining the motor training hypothesis for the evolution of play', *The American Naturalist,* 146(1): 25–40.

Byron, T. (2010) *Do We Have Safer Children in a Digital World? Progress Since the 2008 Byron Review,* http://webarchive.nationalarchives.gov.uk/20100407120701/dcsf.gov.uk/byronreview.

Carey, N. (2012) *The Epigenetics Revolution: How Modern Biology is Rewriting Our Understanding of Genetics, Disease and Inheritance.* London: Icon Books.

Carey, S. (1985) *Conceptual Change in Childhood.* Cambridge, MA: MIT Press.

Chomsky, N. (2006) *Language and Mind.* Cambridge: Cambridge University Press.

Child Exploitation and Online Protection (CEOP) Centre (2015) www.thinkuknow.co.uk/Teachers.

Chouinard, M.M. (2007) 'Children's questions: a mechanism for cognitive development', *Monographs of the Society for the Research in Child Development,* 72: 1–112.

Common Sense Media (2011) *Zero to Eight: Children's Media Use in America,* www.commonsensemedia.org/research/zero-eight-childrensmedia-use-america.

Copley, J. and Padron, Y. (1999) 'Preparing teachers of young learners: professional development of early childhood teachers in mathematics and science', in G.D. Nelson (ed.), *Dialogue on Early Childhood Science, Mathematics and Technology Education.* Washington, DC: American Association for the Advancement of Science, pp. 117–29.

Corentin, P. (2003) *Plouf!* Paris: Ecole des Loisirs.

Crescenzi, L., Jewitt. C. and Price, S. (2014) 'The role of touch in preschool children using iPad versus paper interaction', *Australian Journal of Language and Literacy*, 37(2): 86–95.

de la Fontaine, J. (2014) *The Fables of Jean de la Fontaine*, bilingual edition, English–French. Sleeping Cat Books.

Department for Education (DfE) (2012) *Foundations for Quality. The Independent Review of Early Education and Childcare Qualifications: Nutbrown Review.* Ref: DFE-00068–2012. London: Crown copyright, www.gov.uk/government/ publications.

Department for Education (DfE) (2013a) *More Great Childcare. Raising Quality and Giving Parents More Choice.* January 2013. London: Crown copyright, www. gov.uk/government.

Department for Education (DfE) (2013b) *Early Years Educator (Level 3): Qualifications Criteria.* Ref: NCTL-00107–2013.Crown copyright, www.gov.uk/ government/publications.

Department for Education (DfE) (2013c) *Teachers' Standards (Early Years).* Ref: NCTL-00108–2013. Crown copyright, www.gov.uk/government/publications.

Department for Education (DfE) (2013d) *National Curriculum in England September 2013.* London: Crown copyright, www.gov.uk/government.

Department for Education (DfE) (2014) *Statutory Framework for the Early Years Foundation Stage: Setting the Standards for Learning, Development and Care for Children from Birth to Five.* London: Crown copyright.

DES (1985) *Assessment of Performance Unit. Science Report for Teachers 6: Practical Testing at Ages 11, 13 and 15.* APU.

Dickens, C. (1996) *Hard Times.* Broadview Literary Texts, pp. 41–42.

Duit, R. (2009) *Students' and Teachers' Conceptions and Science Education*, www. ipn.uni-kiel.de/aktuell/stcse/stcse.htm.

Duschl, R.A. and Gitomer, D.H. (1997) 'Strategies and challenges to changing the focus of assessment and instruction in science classrooms', *Educational Assessment*, 4(1): 37–73.

Duschl, R.A., Schweingruber, H. and Shouse, A.W. (2007) *Taking Science to School: Learning and Teaching Science in Grades K-8 Committee on Science Learning, Kindergarten through to Eighth Grade.* Washington, DC: National Research Council of the Academies, The National Academies Press.

Dweck, C.S. (2000) *Self-theories: Their Role in Motivation, Personality and Development.* Philadelphia, PA: Psychology Press.

Edwards, C. and Gandini, L. (2011) *The Hundred Languages of Children: The Reggio Emilia Experience in Transformation.* Westport, CT: Greenwood Press.

Embedded Design Research Laboratory University of California Berkeley (2015) http://edrl.berkeley.edu.

Finnegan, J. and Warren, H. (2015) *Ready to Read. Closing the Gap in Early Language Skills so that Every Child in England Can Read Well.* London: Save the Children.

Fleer, M. and Hardy, T. (2001) 'How can we find out what 3 and 4 years olds think? New approaches to eliciting very young children's understandings in science', *Research in Science Education*, 23(1): 68–76.

Fodor, J.A. (1983) *The Modularity of Mind: An Essay on Faculty Psychology.* Cambridge, MA: MIT Press.

Formby, S. (2014) *Practitioner Perspectives: Children's Use of Technology in the Early Years.* London: National Literacy Trust.

Fortey, R. (1998) *Life, An Unauthorised Autobiography. A Natural History of the First 4,000,000,000 Years of Life on Earth.* London: Flamingo.

Frost, J. (1997) *Creativity in Primary Science.* Maidenhead: Open University Press.

Gelman, S.A. (2003) *The Essential Child: Origins of Essentialism in Everyday Thought.* London: Oxford University Press.

Gelman, R. and Brenneman, K. (2012) 'Moving young scientists in waiting onto science learning pathways: focus on observation', in S.M. Carver and J. Shrager (eds), *The Journey from Child to Scientist: Integrating Cognitive Development and the Education Science.* APA, pp. 155–69.

Gelman, S.A. and Rhodes, M. (2012) 'Two-thousand years of stasis', in K.S. Rosengren, S.K. Brem, E.M. Evans and G.M. Sinatra (eds), *Evolution Challenges: Integrating Research and Practice in Teaching and Learning about Evolution.* Oxford: Oxford University Press.

Goldin-Meadow, S. (2009) 'How gestures promote learning throughout childhood', *Child Development Perspectives,* 3(2): 106–111.

Goodman, A. and Gregg, P. (2010) *Poorer Children's Educational Attainment.* Joseph Rowntree Foundation, www.jrf.org.uk/sites/files/jrf/poorer-children-education-full.pdf.

Greif, M.L., Kemler Nelson, D.G., Keil, F.C. and Gutierrez, F. (2006) 'What do children want to know about animals and artefacts? Domain-specific requests for information', *Psychological Science,* 17(6): 455–59.

Harlen, W. (1997) 'Primary teachers' understanding in science and its impact in the classroom research', *Science Education,* 27(3): 323–37.

Harlen, W. (2008) 'Science as a key component of the primary curriculum: a rationale with policy implications', *Perspectives on Education 1 (Primary Science),* pp. 4–18, www.wellcome.ac.uk/perspectives.

Haughland, S.W. (1999) 'What role should technology play in young children's learning?', *Part 1: Young Children,* 54(6): 26–31. Updated in 2011, www.education.com/reference/article/Ref_Computers_Children/?page=3.

Heft, T.M. and Swaminathan, S. (2002) 'The effects of computers on the social behaviour of pre-schoolers', *Journal of Research in Childhood Education,* 16(2): 162–74.

Higgins, S., Xiao, Z. and Katsipataki, M. (2012) *The Impact of Technology on Learning: A Summary for the Education Endowment Foundation.* Durham: Educational Endowment Foundation and Durham University.

Hoban, B. and Nielsen, W. (2012) 'Learning science through creating a 'Slowmation': a case study of preservice primary teachers', *International Journal of Science Education,* 35(1): 119–46.

Holroyd, C. and Harlen, W. (1996) 'Primary teachers' confidence about teaching science and technology', *Research Papers in Education,* 11(3): 323–35.

Howe, C. (2014) 'Optimising small group discourse in classrooms: effective practices and theoretical constraints', *International Journal of Educational Research,* 63:107–115.

Inagaki, K. and Hatano, G. (2002) *Young Children's Naive Thinking about the Biological World*. New York: Psychology Press.

Inhelder, B. and Piaget, J. (1958) *The Growth of Logical Thinking from Childhood to Adolescence*. London: Routledge.

Inhelder, B. and Piaget, J. (1964) *The Early Growth of Logic in the Child*. London: Routledge.

Isaacs, N. (1962) 'The case for bringing science into the primary school', in W.H. Perkins (ed.), *The Place of Science in Primary Education*. London: British Association for the Advancement of Science.

Kagan, S. and Kagan, M. (2009) *Kagan Cooperative Learning*. Kagan.

Karmiloff-Smith, A. (1995) *Beyond Modularity: Developmental Perspective on Cognitive Science* (Learning, Development and Conceptual Change). Cambridge, MA: MIT Press.

Karmiloff-Smith, A. (2012) 'Is development domain specific or domain general? A third alternative', in S.M. Carver and J. Shrager (eds), *The Journey from Child to Scientist: Integrating Cognitive Development and the Education Science*. APA, pp. 127–40.

Keil, F.C. (2012) 'Does folk science develop?', in S.M. Carver and J. Shrager (eds), *The Journey from Child to Scientist: Integrating Cognitive Development and the Education Science*. APA, pp. 67–86.

Kirkorian, H.L. and Pempek, T.A. (2013) 'Toddlers and touch screens: potential for early learning?', *Zero to Three*, 33: 32–7.

Klahr, D. (2012) 'Patterns, rules and discoveries in life and in science', in S.M. Carver and J. Shrager (eds), *The Journey from Child to Scientist: Integrating Cognitive Development and the Education Science*. APA, pp. 263–92.

Klapproth, D.M. (2004) *Narrative as Social Practice: Anglo-Western and Aboriginal Oral Traditions*. Berlin: Mouton de Gruyter.

Kuhn, D. (2005) *Education for Thinking*. Harvard: Harvard University Press.

Lehrer, R. and Schauble, L. (2012) 'Supporting inquiry about the foundations of evolutionary thinking in the elementary grades', in S.M. Carver and J. Shrager (eds), *The Journey from Child to Scientist*. APA, pp.171–205.

Leibham, M.B., Alexander, J.M. and Johnson, K.E. (2013) 'Science interests in pre-school boys and girls: relations to later self-concept and science achievement', *Science Education*, 97(4): 574–93.

Marmot, M. (2010) *Fair Society, Healthy Lives: The Marmot Review Executive Summary*. London: UCL Institute of Health Equity.

Marmot, M. (2014) *Marmot Indicators 2014. A Preliminary Summary with Graphs. Strategic Review of Health Inequalities Post 2010*. London: UCL Institute of Health Equity September 2014.

McGuigan, L. and Russell, T. (2015) 'Using multimodal strategies to challenge early years children's essentialist beliefs', *Journal of Emergent Science*, 9: 32–43.

McPake, J., Plowman, L. and Stephen, C. (2013) 'Pre-school children creating and communicating with digital technologies in the home', *British Journal of Educational Technology*, 44(3): 421–31.

Mercer, N. (2013) 'The social brain, language, and goal-directed collective thinking: a social conception of cognition and its implications for understanding how we think, teach, and learn', *Educational Psychologist*, 48(3): 148–68.

Mercer, N. and Howe, C. (2012) 'Explaining the dialogic processes of teaching and learning: the value of sociocultural theory', *Learning, Culture and Social Interaction,* 1(1): 12–21.

Milbourne, A. (2012) *The Windy Day.* London: Usborne Publishing.

Murphy, C. and Beggs, J. (2005) *Primary Science in the UK: A Scoping Study. Final report to the Wellcome Trust.* London: Wellcome Trust.

National Institute for Health and Care Excellence (NICE) (2015) *Maintaining a Healthy Weight and Preventing Excess Weight Gain Among Adults and Children.* NICE Guidelines NG7.

National Society for Protection of Cruelty to Children (NSPCC) (2015) www.nspcc.org.uk/preventing-abuse/keeping-children-safe/online-safety.

Naylor, S. and Keogh, B. (2013) *Concept Cartoons In Science Education* (2nd edn). Sandbach: Millgate House Publishers.

Norris, P.M., Guilbert, S.M., Smith, M.L., Hakimelahi, S. and Phillips, L.M. (2005) 'A theoretical framework for narrative explanation in science', *Science Education,* 89(4).

Ofcom (2014) *Children and Parents: Media Use and Attitudes.* Ofcom independent regulator and competition authority for communications industries report, October, http://stakeholders.ofcom.org.uk/market-data-research/other/research-publications/childrens/children-parents-oct-14.

Papert, S. (1994) *The Children's Machine: Rethinking School in the Age of the Computer.* Basic Books: New York.

Piaget, J. (1973) *The Child and Reality: Problems of Genetic Psychology.* New York: Grossman Publishers.

Pinker, S. (2013) *Language, Cognition and Human Nature* (1st edn). New York: OUP.

Plakitsi, K. (2013) *Activity Theory in Formal and Informal Science Education.* Rotterdam/Boston/Taipei: Sense Publishers.

Roth, W.-M. (2013) *Meaning and Mental Representation: A Pragmatic Approach.* Rotterdam, The Netherlands: Sense Publishers.

Roth, W.-M., Goulart, M.I.M. and Plakitsi, K. (2013) *Science During Early Childhood: A Cultural-Historical Perspective.* Dordrecht, The Netherlands: Springer.

Russell, T. (2011) 'Progression in learning science', in W. Harlen (ed.), *ASE Guide to Primary Science.* Hatfield: Association for Science Education, pp. 17–24.

Russell, T. (2015a) 'Multimodal representations and science learning', in R. Gunstone (ed.), *Encyclopedia of Science Education,* Heidelberg/New York/London: Springer Dordrecht, pp. 673–80.

Russell, T. (2015b) 'Developmental perspectives on learning', in R. Gunstone (ed.), *Encyclopedia of Science Education.* Heidelberg/New York/London: Springer Dordrecht, pp. 297–300.

Russell, T. and McGuigan, L. (2003) 'Promoting understanding through representational redescription: an illustration referring to young pupils' ideas about gravity', in D. Psillos, P. Kariotoglou, V. Tselfes, E. Hatzikraniotis, G. Fassoulopoulos and M. Kallery (eds), *Science Education Research in the Knowledge-based Society.* Dordrecht/Boston/London: Kluwer, pp. 277–84.

Russell, T. and McGuigan, L. (2005) *INSET Toolkit for Key Stages 1, 2 and 3. Assessing Progress in Science*. London: Qualifications and Curriculum Authority (QCA), ISBN 85838–721–3 (KS1), ISBN 85838–722–1(KS2), ISBN 85838–723–X (KS3).

Russell, T. and McGuigan, L. (2016) 'Identifying and enhancing the science within early years holistic practice', in N. Papadouris, A. Hadjigeorgiou and C. Constantinou (eds), *Insights from Research in Science Teaching and Learning*. Cham, Switzerland: Springer International Publishing, pp. 187–200.

Sacks, O. (1985) *The Man Who Mistook his Wife for a Hat and Other Clinical Tales*. Summit Books.

Seehra, J.S. Verma, A. Peppler, K. and Ramani, K. (2015*) Handimate: Create and Animate Using Everyday Objects as Material*. TEI 2015 proceedings of the Ninth International Conference on Tangible, Embedded and Embodied Interaction, January 15–19, CA: Stanford University.

Segal, A. (2011) 'Do gestural interfaces promote thinking? Embodied interaction: congruent gestures and direct touch performance in math', submitted in partial fulfilment of the requirements for the degree of Doctor of Philosophy under the Executive committee of the Graduate School of Arts and Science Columbia University.

Shayer, M. and Adey, P. (1981) *Towards a Science of Science Teaching*. London: Heinemann.

Shayer, M, Denise Ginsburg, D. and Coe, R. (2007) 'Thirty years on – a large anti-Flynn effect? The Piagetian test volume and heaviness norms 1975–2003', *British Journal of Educational Psychology*, 77: 25–41.

Shulman, L.S. (1987) 'Knowledge and teaching: foundations of the new reform', *Harvard Educational Review*, 7(1): 1–22.

Simon, S., Naylor, S., Keogh, B., Maloney, J. and Downing, B. (2008) 'Puppets promoting engagement and talk in science', *International Journal of Science Education*, 30(9): 1229–48.

Sinnott-Armstrong, W. and Fogelin, R.J. (2010) *Understanding Arguments: An Introduction to Informal Logic*. USA: Wadsworth Cengage Learning.

Stylianidou, F. and Agogi, E. (2014) *Enabling Creativity through Science and Mathematics in Preschool and First Years of Primary Education (CLS)*. Final Project Report. EU.

Tandon, P.S., Zhou, C., Lozano, P. and Christakis. D.A. (2011) 'Preschoolers' total daily screen time at home and by type of child care', *Journal of Pediatrics*, 158(2): 297–300.

Thulin, S. and Pramling, N. (2009) 'Anthropomorphically speaking: on communication between teachers and children in early childhood biology education', *International Journal of Early Years Education*, 17(2): 137–50.

Turner, J., Keogh, B., Naylor, S. and Lawrence, E. (2011) *It's Not Fair – or Is It? A Guide to Developing Children's Ideas through Primary Science Enquiry*. Sandbach: Millgate House Publishers.

UK Council for Child Internet Safety (UKCCIS) (2015) Research summaries from the evidence group of the UKCCIS, February, www.saferinternet.org.

Vosniadou, S. (2013) *International Handbook of Research on Conceptual Change* (2nd edn). New York: Routledge.

Vygotsky, L. (1962) *Thought and Language*. Cambridge, MA: MIT Press.

Vygotsky, L. (1978) *Mind in Society*. Cambridge, MA: Harvard University Press.

Watson, J. (1999) *The Double Helix: A Personal Account of the Discovery of the Structure of DNA* (2nd edn). London: Penguin.

Watson, R., Goldsworthy, A. and Wood Robinson, V. (1998) *AKSIS Project, Second Interim Report to the QCA*. London: Kings College.

Watt, D. and Russell, T. (1990) *Sound Primary Science Process and Concept Exploration Research Report*. Liverpool: Liverpool University Press.

Westermann, G., Thomas, M. and Karmiloff-Smith, A. (2010) 'Neuroconstructivism', in U. Goswami (ed.), *Handbook of Childhood Cognitive Development*. Oxford: Wiley-Blackwell, pp. 723–48.

Willis, J. and Ross, T. (2003) *The Tadpole's Promise*. London: Random House.

Wilson, M. (2008) 'How did we get from there to here? An evolutionary perspective on embodied cognition', in P. Calvo, and A. Gomila (eds), *Handbook of Cognitive Science: An Embodied Approach*. San Diego, CA: Elsevier Science.

Wormell, C. (2011) *One Smart Fish*. London: Red Fox Picture Books.

Index